# Working It
Food for the Workweek

## in the Kitchen

**KIM BAKER**

This book was developed in the evenings after a full workday in between washing dishes, doing laundry and overseeing bathtime.
Each recipe is crafted based on the ambition, accessibility and needs of those doing their best to bring good food to their homes, friends and family after a long day of work.

I share it with you because I believe in its importance.
Make dinnertime your own.

*In celebration of a man lost, but a spirit that remains.
Nicholas Croce, my Picasso.*

∞

Working It in the Kitchen™: Food for the Workweek
Copyright ©2014 by Picasso Foods, LLC.
First edition.
All rights reserved. Printed in the United States of America. No part of this book may be used or reproduced in any matter whatsoever without written permission except in the case of brief quotations embodied in critical articles and reviews.

For information, visit:
www.facebook.com/kimbakerfoods

Cover and lifestyle photo credit to Paige Stevens Photography.
www.paigestevens.com

PICASSO FOOD™

# CONTENTS

Preface vii

Happy & Healthy
Main Dishes
1

Fast & Fabulous
Side Dishes
31

Pantry Dive™
61

Splurge
83

Your own story will provide context to these pages.
At the center of mine, is a sandy-haired gift given to me
amid less than perfect circumstances.
Work has never been more relevant –
the energy, input, displacement and weariness
balanced by a magnitude of joy and reward.

And in the kitchen...I continue to work it.

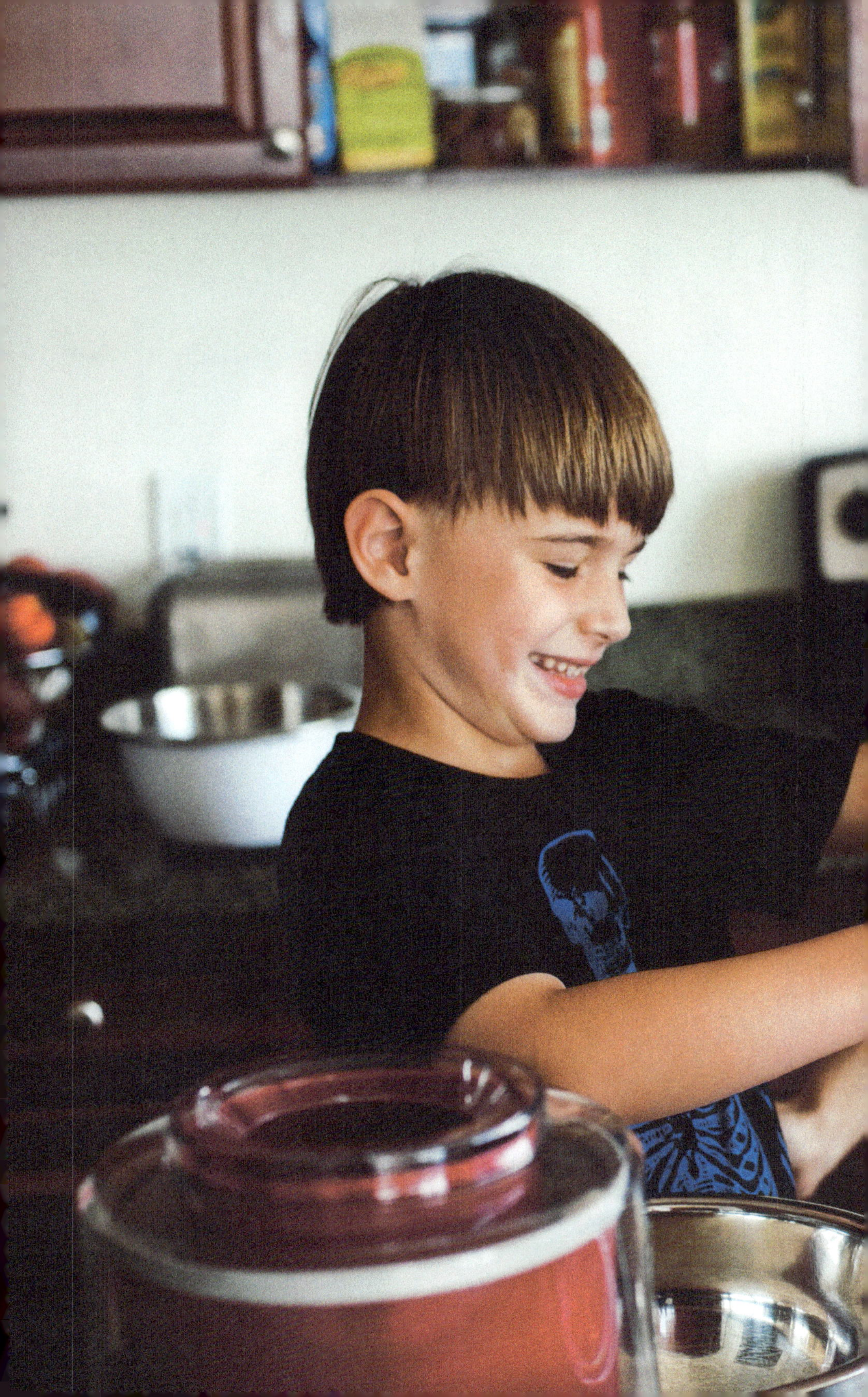

Organic Pasture-Raised
pyrex
500 ml
450
400 ml
350
300 ml
250
200 ml

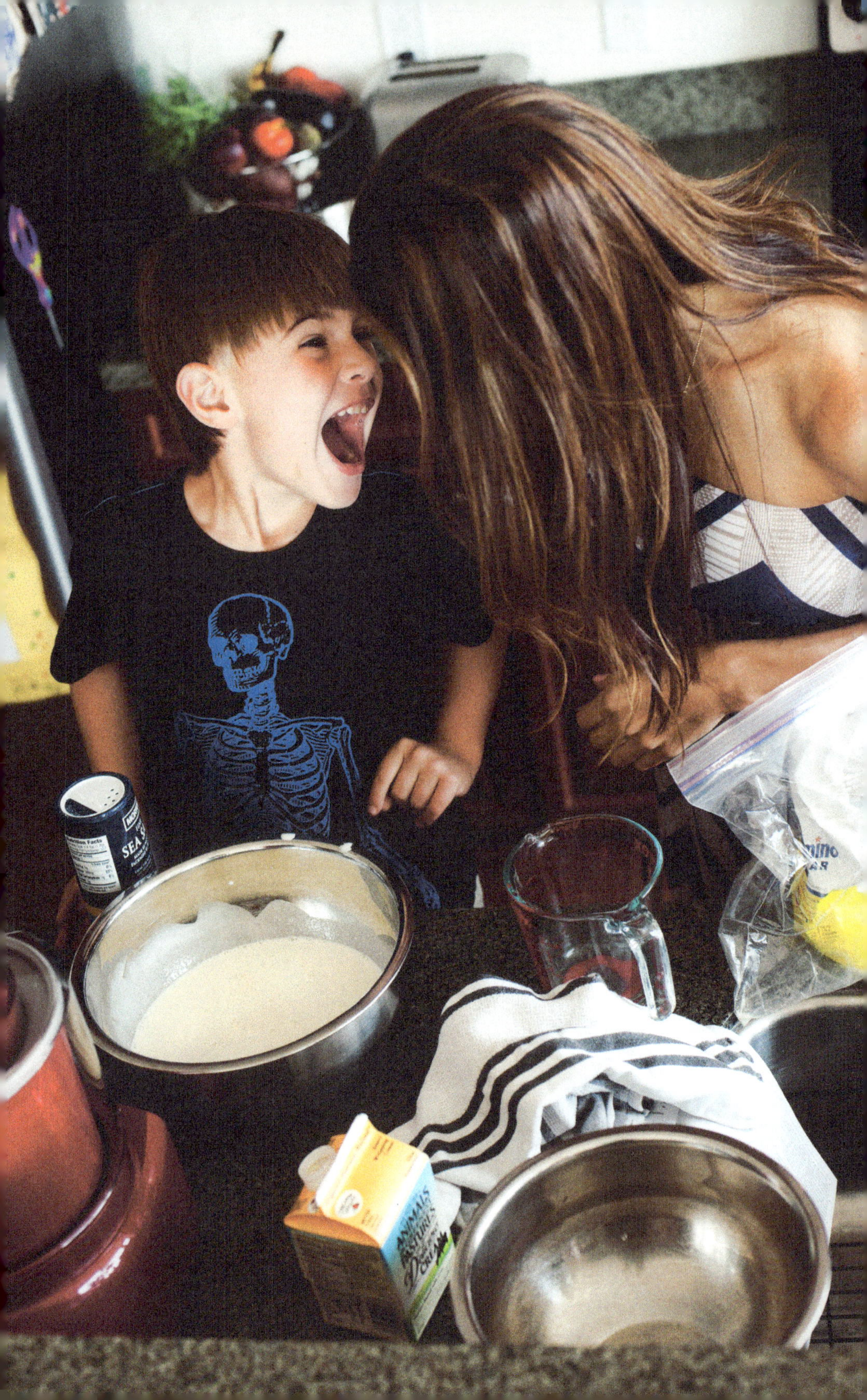

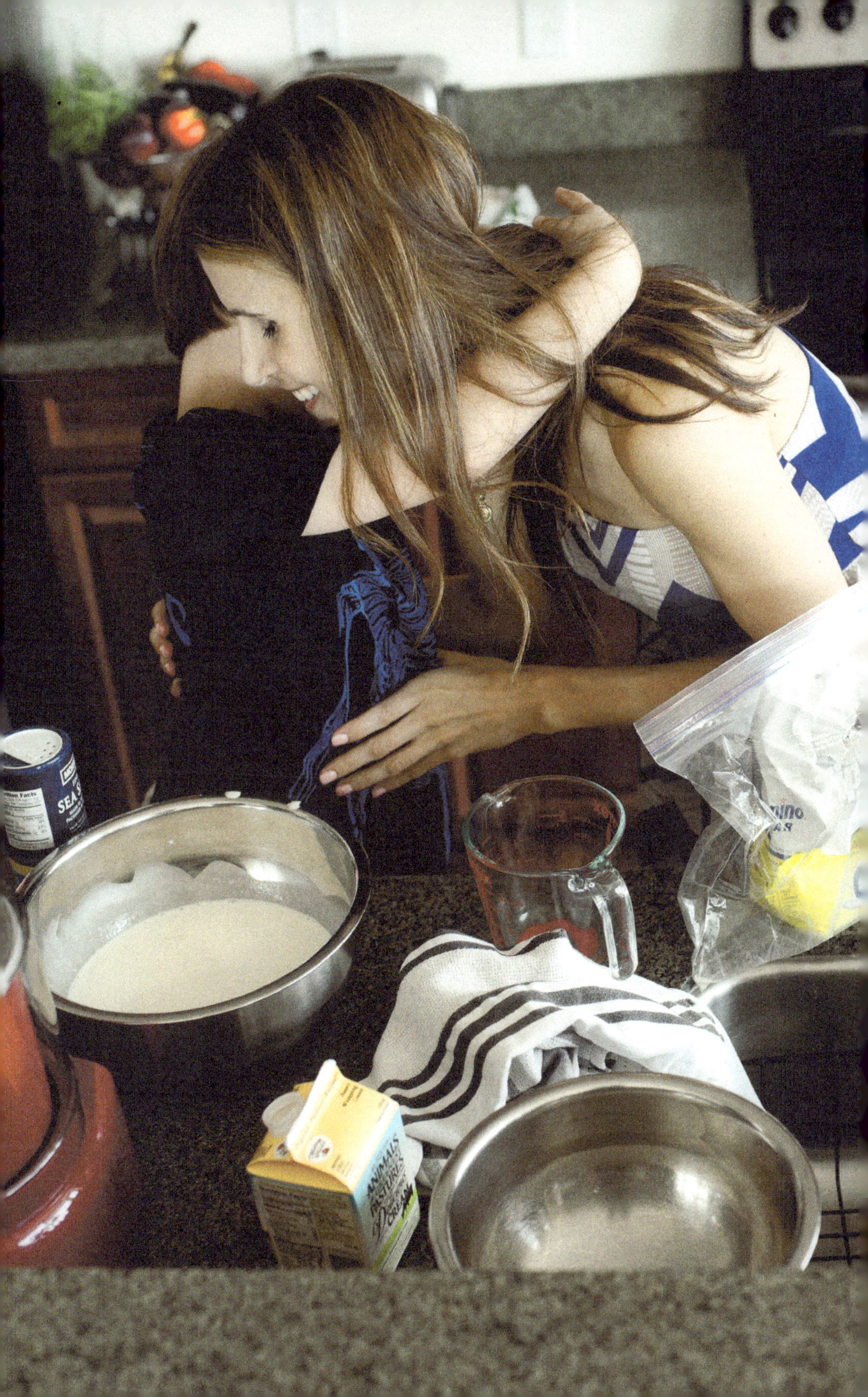

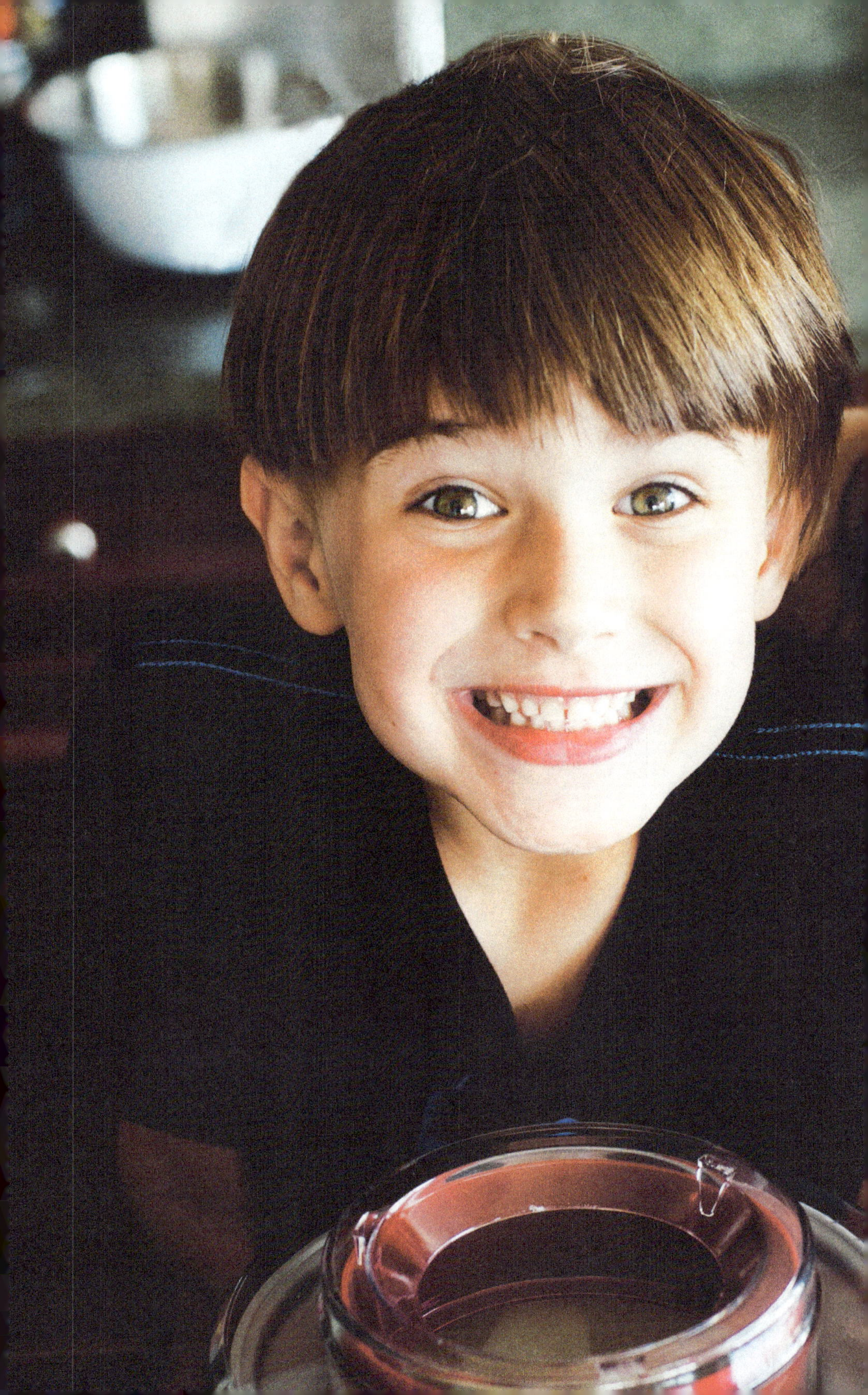

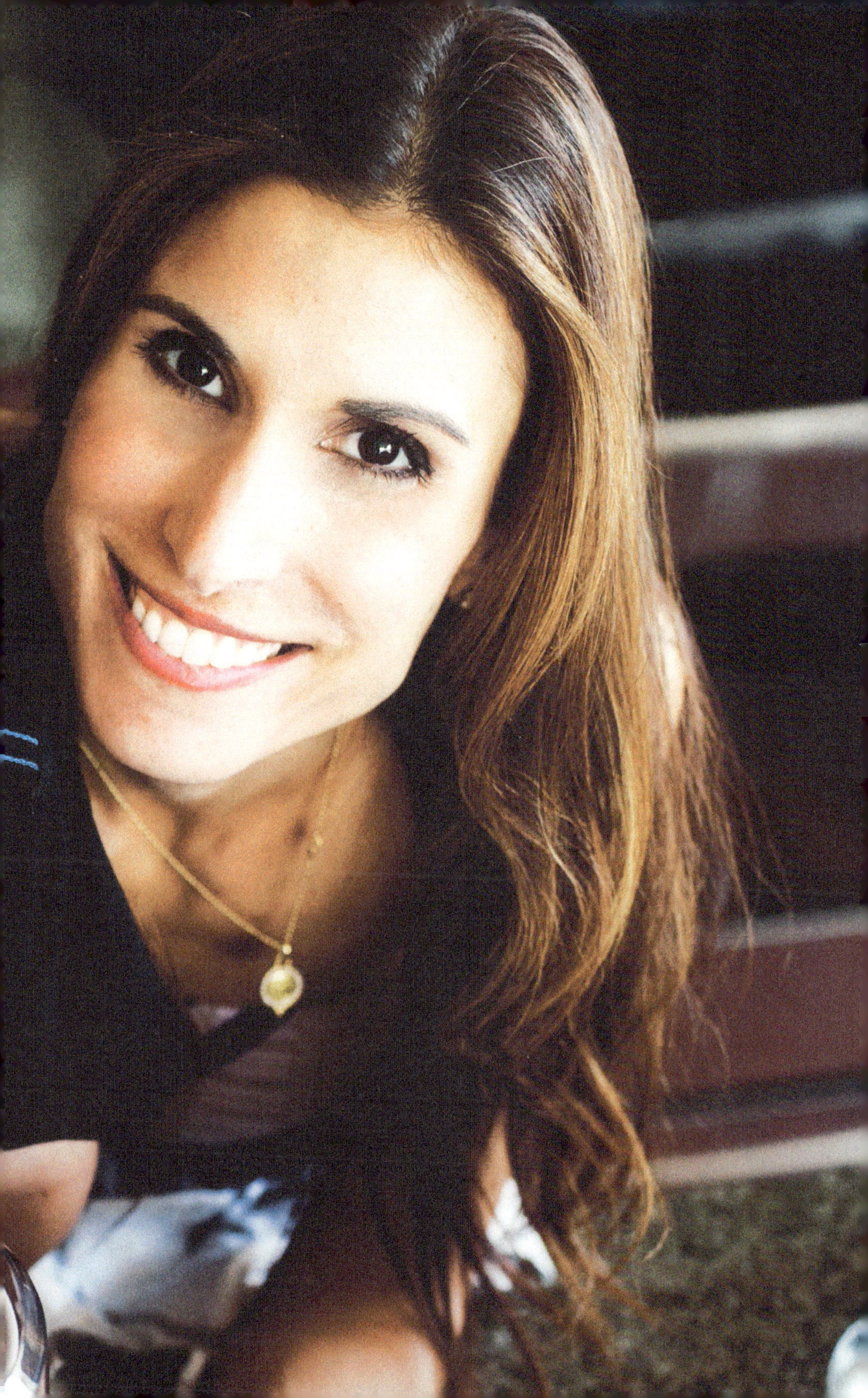

# Working It™

## happy & healthy: mains

| | |
|---|---|
| 4 | Pineapple Pork Chops |
| 5 | *Leftover Idea:* Open Pork Sandwiches with Kale and Basil |
| 5 | *Leftover Idea:* Cuban Pork Quesadillas |
| 6 | Chicken Thighs with Sweet Potatoes |
| 7 | Margarita Shrimp |
| 8 | Ravioli with Asparagus in Butter Wine Sauce |
| 9 | Creamy Linguini with Cod and Basil |
| 10 | Pasta with Mushroom Meat Sauce |
| 11 | *Leftover Idea:* Savory Beans and Rice |
| 11 | *Leftover Idea:* Eggplant Wraps |
| 12 | Chilean Sea Bass with Fennel and Zucchini |
| 13 | Brazil Nut-Crusted Salmon |
| 14 | Steak Fajitas Sans Tortillas |
| 15 | Breaded Chicken Breast Cutlets |
| 16 | Mahi-Mahi with Asparagus, Tomatoes and Olives |
| 17 | Chicken Patties with Ricotta |
| 18 | Beet, Feta and Arugula Quesadillas |
| 19 | Lemon Tilapia |
| 20 | Cod with Sautéed Spinach |
| 21 | *Leftover Idea:* Asian Fish Biscuits |
| 22 | *Leftover Idea:* Fish Tacos |
| 22 | Pasta with Sausage, Fennel and Tomatoes |
| 23 | Sweet and Simple Pork Cutlets |
| 24 | Roasted Chicken with Apples and Celery |
| 25 | *Leftover Idea:* BBQ Chicken and Apple Pizza |
| 25 | *Leftover Idea:* Apple Walnut Chicken Salad |
| 26 | Turkey Burgers with Brie and Sauteed Apples |
| 27 | Seared Scallops with Cabbage |
| 28 | Crispy Pan-Seared Salmon |
| 29 | *Leftover Idea:* Salmon and Cabbage Salad |
| 29 | *Leftover Idea:* Salmon Cakes |

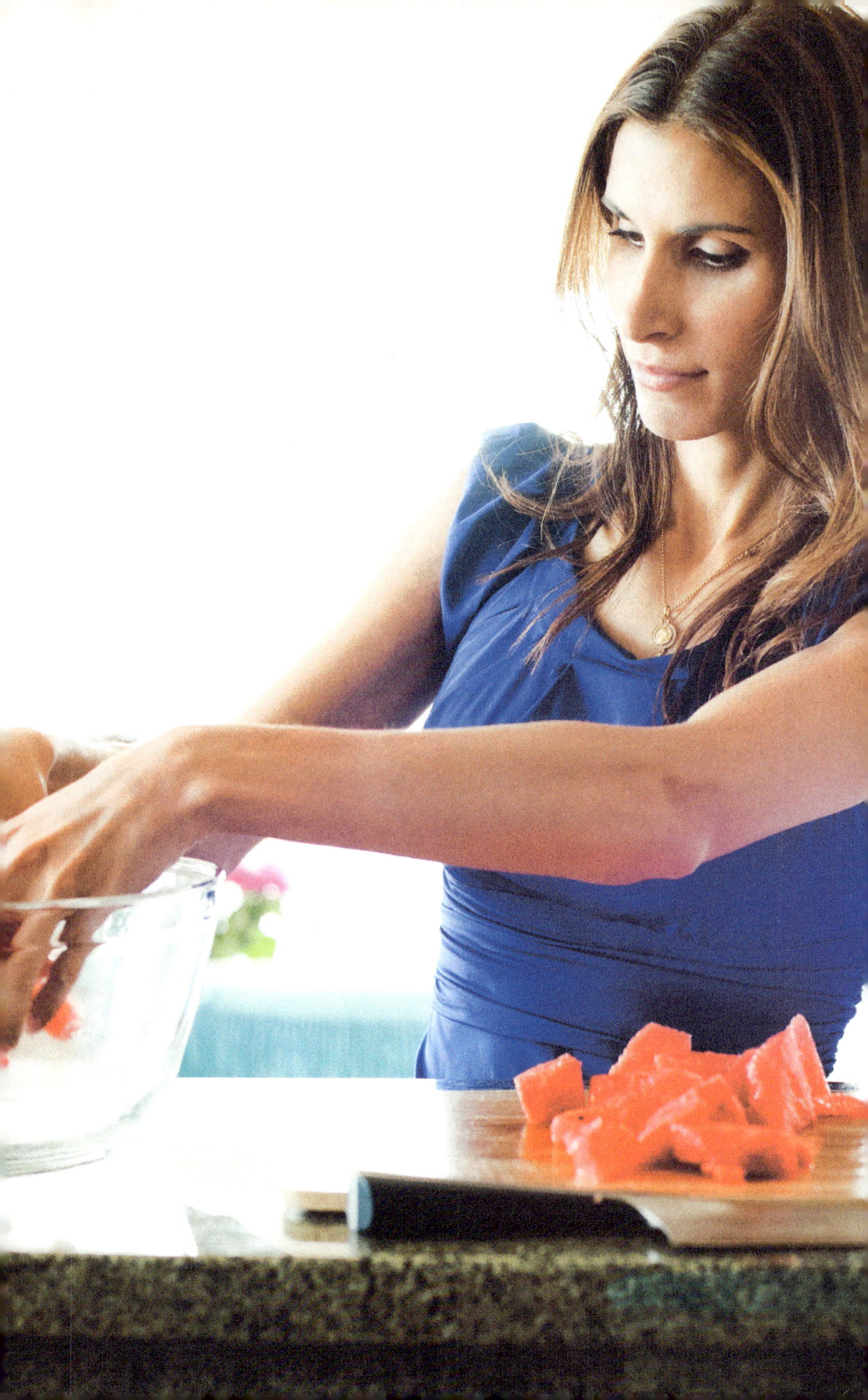

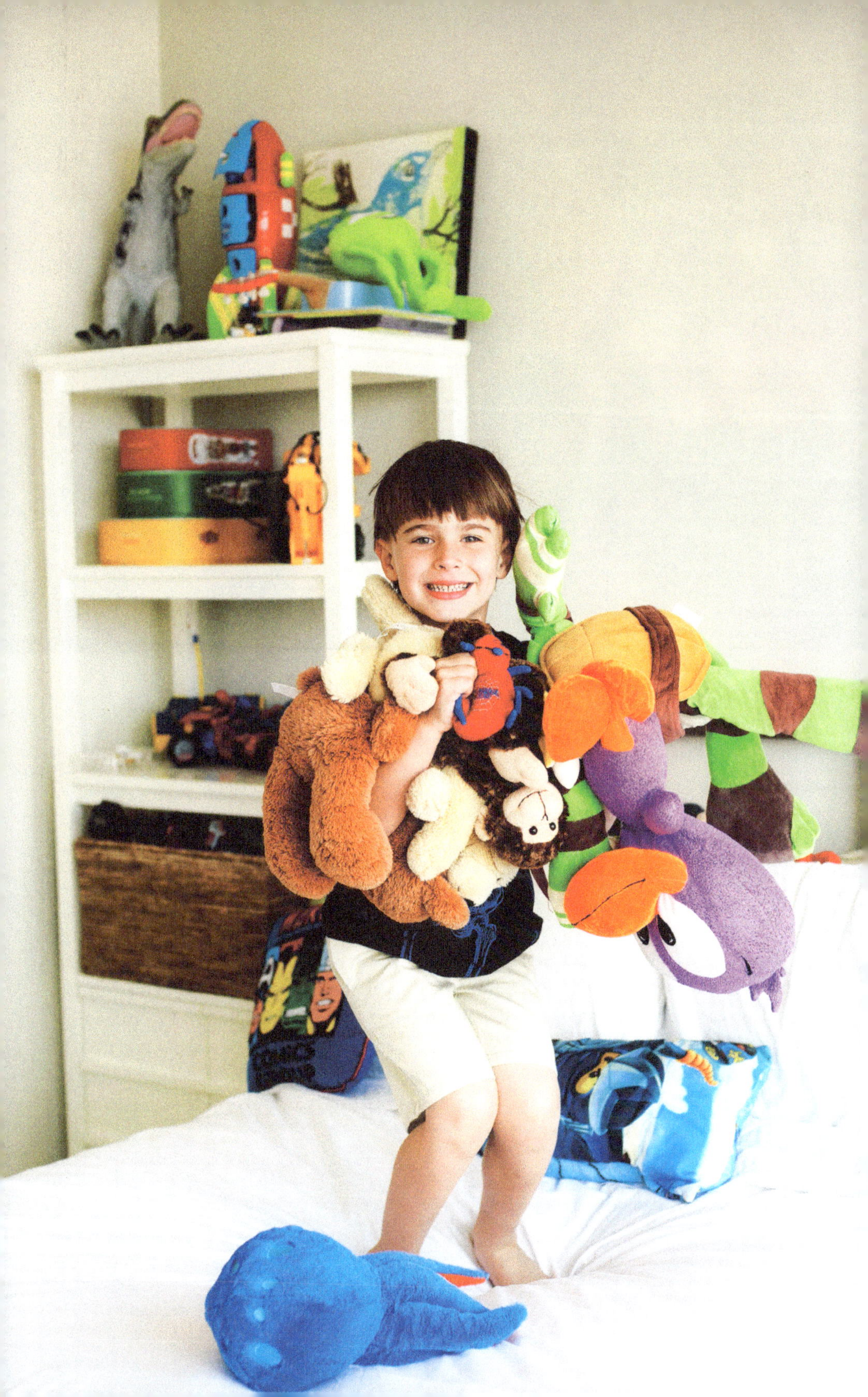

*So good, it may be worthy of becoming a part of your weekly routine.*

## Pineapple Pork Chops

**Ingredients**

2 t. olive oil
four boneless pork chops (approximately 1 lb.)
1 T. grainy mustard
1/2 t. cinnamon
1/8 t. garlic powder

1 T. plus 1 t. brown sugar
sea salt and pepper
six pineapple slices
1 T. molasses

Preheat oven to 400 degrees. Spread olive oil in roasting pan. Rub both sides of pork with mustard, cinnamon, garlic powder, 1 T. brown sugar, salt and pepper. Place in roasting pan and top each with a pineapple slice. Chop remaining slices of pineapple plus 1 t. brown sugar and add to roasting pan around pork. If there is any juice from the pineapple, add it to the pan as well. Drizzle pork with molasses and cook for approximately 30 minutes, depending on thickness, until just cooked through. Remove pork from pan and drizzle with pan juices.

Serves 4.

Fresh pineapple is best and worth the effort, but if need be, use an 8 oz. can.

## LEFTOVERS
### Open Pork Sandwiches with Kale and Basil

baguette (4" long)
cooking spray
one kale leaf, center rib and stem removed
sea salt
one leftover Pineapple Pork Chop
basil, approx. 4 large leaves
approx. 1/4 C. fontina cheese (or whatever's on-hand)

Heat broiler. Slice baguette open and spray inside generously with cooking spray. Place on aluminum foil and broil 1-2 minutes until golden. Remove from oven. Tear kale and place on each half of bread and season with salt. Slice pork thinly and place on top. Add 2 slices of basil, half a pineapple slice and 1/8 C. cheese to each half. Place back in oven open-faced for approximately 2 minutes until cheese is melted and bubbly.

## LEFTOVERS    Cuban Pork Quesadillas

one tortilla, burrito sized
cooking spray
3/4 t. mayo
1/8 t. mustard
1/4 t. honey
four round pickle slices
half a leftover Pineapple Pork Chop
1/8 C. cheddar cheese

Spray tortilla with cooking spray and place spray-side down in heated skillet. Mix mayo, mustard and honey in small bowl and spread lightly over tortilla. Add pickles, chopped pork chop and pineapple on one-half side of tortilla. Sprinkle with cheese. Fold over. Cook 2 minutes, flip and cook additional 2 minutes until both sides are golden.

## Chicken Thighs with Sweet Potatoes

**Ingredients**

four chicken thighs, bone-in with skin
sea salt and pepper
3 large sweet potatoes, peeled and cubed
1/2 C. vidalia onion, sliced

1/4 C. white wine
1/4 C. chicken stock
1/8 C. basil, chopped
2 t. balsamic vinegar

Heat a large non-stick skillet over medium heat. Pat chicken dry with paper towel, season each piece with salt and pepper, and place in pan skin-side down. Cook 4 minutes and flip. Add potatoes and onions. Let cook approximately 5-6 minutes until potatoes have browned slightly. Add wine and stock. Cover and let cook 12-15 minutes until chicken is cooked through. Remove from oven and add basil and balsamic.

Serves 4.

This dish can also be made with chicken breasts, but you'll need to cook the chicken longer before adding the potatoes. White potatoes can also be used in place of or in addition to the sweet potatoes.

**Fiesta time.**

# Margarita Shrimp

**Ingredients**

1 1/2 lb. uncooked shrimp, peeled and deveined
1 t. olive oil
sea salt and pepper
1/4 t. garlic powder
1/4 t. paprika

3 T. butter
juice of one orange
juice of half a lime
2 T. cilantro, coarsely chopped

In a large bowl, combine shrimp with olive oil, salt, pepper, garlic powder and paprika. Melt 1 T. butter in a large skillet over medium to medium-high heat. Add half of shrimp to pan and let cook 2 minutes, flip, and cook for an additional minute until cooked through. Remove shrimp from pan and set aside. Repeat with 1 T. butter and remaining shrimp. Add all shrimp back to pan, and add orange juice, lime juice, cilantro and remaining 1T. butter.

Serves 4.

Scallops are a great alternative.
If you don't have cilantro, parsley is a good substitute.

## Ravioli with Asparagus in Butter Wine Sauce

**Ingredients**

one dozen ravioli
1 t. olive oil
1/2 C. red onion, thinly sliced
one bunch of asparagus, ends trimmed, and cut into thirds

sea salt and pepper
1 1/2 C. chicken broth
3/4 C. white wine
4 T. butter

Prepare ravioli according to directions and drain. Meanwhile, heat olive oil in large skillet over medium heat. Add onions and asparagus. Sauté 3-4 minutes until softened and lightly browned. Season with salt and pepper. Add broth and white wine, bring to boil and reduce heat. Add butter. Season with salt and pepper to taste. Let sit 2-3 minutes to thicken, and add ravioli.

Serves 4.

This sauce is delicious and can be used with other pastas, such as spaghetti. It is also terrific with grilled chicken or fish.

# Creamy Linguini with Cod and Basil

Ingredients

1 lb. pasta, such as linguini
2 t. olive oil
12 oz. cod, cut into 2" cubes
sea salt and pepper
1/2 C. chicken stock

1 3/4 C. low-fat milk
1/2 C. half-and-half
2 t. butter
1/8 C. basil, chopped

Prepare pasta according to directions and drain. Meanwhile, heat olive oil in large skillet over medium heat. Season cod with salt and pepper, and add to skillet. Cook for 1-2 minutes, flip, and cook for an additional 1-2 minutes. Add chicken broth, milk and half-and-half. Bring to boil and reduce heat. Add butter and additional salt and pepper and let cook 3-4 minutes. Sauce will still be thin. Add pasta and basil to sauce, and let sit over low heat for 5 minutes to incorporate flavor and absorb sauce.

Serves 6.

This dish can also be prepared with shrimp.
Using stock and low-fat milk keeps the sauce light.

# Pasta with Mushroom Meat Sauce

**Ingredients**

1 lb. pasta, such as spaghetti or ziti
1 T. olive oil
two shallots, finely chopped
1/8 t. red pepper flakes
16 oz. mushrooms, sliced

1 lb. lean ground beef
sea salt and pepper
one 14.5 oz. can diced tomato
one 15 oz. can tomato sauce
3 T. parmesan cheese, grated

Prepare pasta according to directions and drain. Meanwhile, heat olive oil in a large skillet over medium heat. Add shallots and red pepper, and sauté for 1-2 minutes. Add mushrooms, and sauté for 3-4 minutes until tender. Add beef to pan and using a fork, break the meat into small pieces. Season with salt and sauté for 3-4 minutes until nearly cooked through. Add diced tomato and let cook for 2 minutes. Smash the diced tomatoes a bit with the back of a fork and add tomato sauce. Season with additional salt and pepper. Reduce heat to low and let cook 5 minutes. Add cheese and stir to combine. Combine sauce with cooked pasta.

Serves 6.

> Substitute a mixture of pork, veal and beef, or ground turkey or chicken. The sauce is very versatile, so make half the pasta (or double the sauce) and use the extra sauce for the left-over ideas on the next page.

## LEFTOVERS
### Savory Beans and Rice

one 15.5 oz. can cannellini beans, lightly rinsed and drained
sea salt and pepper
approx. 1 1/2 C. leftover Mushroom Meat Sauce (without the pasta)
approx. 1/4 C. water
approx. 3 C. cooked rice
approx. 1/2 C. cheddar cheese, grated

Add beans to a skillet over medium heat. Season with pinch of salt and pepper. Add Mushroom Meat Sauce and water to pan. Let cook 5 minutes. To serve plate 3/4 C. rice, top with a quarter of beef mixture and 1/8 C. cheese, and microwave for 45 seconds until melted. Alternatively, put rice in a pan, layer with beef mixture and then cheese, and broil for 1 minute.

## LEFTOVERS    Eggplant Wraps

See recipe for Parmesan Crusted Eggplant on page 36 except cut eggplant lengthwise into long strips, and stop before adding the parmesan cheese at the end.

approx. 3/4 C. leftover Mushroom Meat Sauce (without the pasta)
approx. 1/3 C. ricotta
approx. 1/4 c. parmesan cheese

Follow instructions for eggplant recipe as indicated above. Once eggplant is tender, remove pan from the oven and add 1 T. meat sauce to one end of each slice of eggplant. Top each with a dollop of ricotta. Roll the eggplant beginning at the filled end. Bake for 6-8 minutes and top with parmesan cheese.

11

**Fish worth craving.**

## Chilean Sea Bass with Fennel and Zucchini

**Ingredients**

1 T. olive oil
one small fennel bulb, sliced thinly
two small zucchini, halved and sliced
four 4-6 oz. chilean sea bass fillets, skin removed

sea salt and pepper
1/2 C. orange juice
2 t. butter

Heat 2 t. olive oil in a large non-stick skillet over medium heat. Add fennel and zucchini, and sauté 3-4 minutes until lightly browned. Push to side of pan. Pat fish dry and season each fillet with salt and pepper. Add remaining 1 t. olive oil to pan and then the fish. Cook 4-5 minutes, flip, and cook for an additional 4-5 minutes. Add orange juice and butter to pan. Season with salt and pepper. Let cook approximately 1 minute allowing juice to reduce.

Serves 4.

Cooking the fennel mellows its flavor. This dish is outstanding and simple to prepare.

Yes, por favor.

## Brazil Nut-Crusted Salmon

**Ingredients**

cooking spray
four 4 oz. salmon fillets
sea salt and pepper

2 T. apricot preserves
10 brazil nuts
one lemon

Preheat oven to 400 degrees. Place salmon skin-side down on a pan generously coated with cooking spray. Season salmon fillets evenly with salt and pepper. Spread 1 1/2 t. apricot preserves on top of each fillet. Put Brazil nuts in a clear plastic bag, and with a can, crush the nuts into coarse pieces. Sprinkle crushed nuts onto the top of the fish, approximately 2 t. per fillet. Place in oven and let cook 12 minutes. Remove from oven and sprinkle lemon juice over top.

Serves 4.

If you don't have apricot preserves, use equal parts of honey and mustard. Brazil nuts are extremely healthy and provide a great crunch.

# Steak Fajitas Sans Tortillas

**Ingredients**

1.75 lb. london broil
1 1/2 t. adobo seasoning
1 1/2 t. olive oil
one red pepper, sliced
half of a red onion, thinly sliced
one pint mushrooms, sliced
1/4 C. barbecue sauce

Season both sides of London broil evenly with 1 t. adobo seasoning and set aside. Heat 1 t. olive oil in a large non-stick skillet over medium heat. Add red pepper and cook 1 minute. Add onion and sauté 5 minutes, then add mushrooms and cook for an additional 4-5 minutes. Season with remaining 1/2 t. adobo. Remove from pan and cover with foil. In the same pan, heat 1/2 t. olive oil and add London broil. Cook for approximately 4-5 minutes on each side for medium rare. Add barbecue sauce, spreading over both sides, and cook for approximately 30 seconds on each side. Remove from heat, let rest, and slice. Serve with vegetables.

Serves 4.

Adobo is a great flavorful seasoning that you can use in all kinds of dishes. You can also make this with other cuts of beef, such as flank steak. Serve with crumbled Feta cheese for a little surprise flavor.

**Winner, winner.**

## Breaded Chicken Breast Cutlets

**Ingredients**

2 eggs
1/4 C. light sour cream
1 C. panko breadcrumbs

1/2 C. italian seasoned breadcrumbs
1/4 C. canola oil
1 lb. chicken breast cutlets

Preheat oven to 450 degrees. Beat eggs lightly with a fork in a small bowl. Add sour cream and beat well to combine. In a separate small bowl, combine panko and Italian seasoned breadcrumbs. Coat a large baking sheet well with oil, covering entire surface. Dip chicken cutlets into egg mixture, coating well, one at a time. Transfer cutlets into the bowl with the breadcrumb mixture and dredge until covered completely. Place in pan. Repeat until all cutlets have been prepared. Cook for 4-6 minutes until bottom of cutlets are golden brown. Remove from oven, flip, and cook for an additional 4-6 minutes to brown the other side.

Serves 4.

You can also prepare broccoli or cauliflower florets, or slices of zucchini like this. Just adjust cooking time accordingly.

## Mahi-Mahi with Asparagus, Tomatoes and Olives

**Ingredients**

four 4-6 oz. mahi-mahi filets, skin removed
sea salt and pepper
12-16 thin asparagus spears, ends trimmed
1/2 C. grape tomatoes, halved

1/4 C. olives, coarsely chopped
2 t. olive oil
one lemon, quartered

Preheat oven to 400 degrees. Cut four large 14" sheets of parchment paper. Place one piece on a baking sheet. Add a slice of fish, seasoned with salt and pepper. Add 3-4 asparagus spears, 1/8 C. tomatoes and 1 T. olives. Drizzle with 1/2 t. olive oil and squeeze one lemon quarter over top. Put squeezed lemon in parchment paper. Wrap parchment to close. Repeat with remaining fish filets. Place in oven and cook 13-15 minutes.

Serves 4.

This recipe is great for any flaky white fish.
Try it with halibut, sea bass, snapper, trout or cod.

## Chicken Patties with Ricotta

Ingredients

1 lb. ground chicken
sea salt and pepper
1/2 C. water
1/4 C. italian seasoned breadcrumbs

1/8 t. garlic powder
2 T. parmesan cheese
2 t. olive oil
1/2 C. ricotta

In a large bowl, combine chicken, salt, pepper, water, breadcrumbs, garlic powder and parmesan cheese. Combine well. Heat 1 t. olive oil in a large skillet over medium heat. Form one quarter of the chicken mixture into a patty and place in skillet. Form a second patty and add to skillet. Let cook 5 minutes on each side until cooked through and remove from heat, keeping covered with foil to stay warm. Add remaining 1 t. olive oil and add two more patties to skillet. Serve each patty with 1/8 C. dollop of warmed ricotta.

Serves 4.

> Serve with a little tomato sauce if you have any on-hand for an easy version of chicken parmesan.

*Taking quesadillas past the border.*

# Beet, Feta and Arugula Quesadillas

**Ingredients**

four burrito sized tortillas
cooking spray
one 16 oz. jar sliced pickled beets
6 oz. feta cheese, crumbled

2 C. arugula
1/2 C. light sour cream
2 t. honey

Spray one side of each tortilla with cooking spray. Place one tortilla sprayed-side down onto a skillet over medium heat. Add about 10 slices of beets, then one quarter of the feta cheese and 1/2 C. arugula. Top with additional tortilla, sprayed-side up. Let cook 2-3 minutes and using a spatula, gently flip. Let cook an additional 2-3 minutes until golden on both sides. Repeat with remaining tortillas.

Serves 2-4

Think beyond beans and salsa, and quesadillas can become a quick and delicious cooking adventure.

# Lemon Tilapia

**Ingredients**

1/3 C. flour
1/4 t. sea salt and pepper, plus pinch
1/4 t. garlic powder
four tilapia fillets
1 T. olive oil

2/3 C. white wine
1 1/4 C. chicken stock
juice of 1 lemon
2 T. butter

In a medium bowl, combine flour with 1/4 t. salt, pepper and garlic powder. Dredge tilapia in flour, coating well. Reserve flour mixture. Heat 1 1/2 t. olive oil in a large skillet over medium heat. Add two pieces of tilapia to pan. Cook for 3-4 minutes, flip, and cook an additional 3-4 minutes until cooked through. Remove from pan and repeat. In the same pan, melt 1 T. butter. Add 2 1/2 t. of reserved flour, blending until incorporated. Add wine and cook 1-2 minutes. Add stock, lemon and remaining butter, and cook 2-3 minutes until thickened. Add tilapia back to pan and flip gently to coat in juices. Season with salt and pepper.

Serves 4.

A delicious, healthy dinner. Tilapia is an easy-to-find and inexpensive fish.

# Cod with Sautéed Spinach

**Ingredients**

1 1/2 t. olive oil
2 garlic cloves, finely chopped
six cups spinach, stems removed
1 T. butter

sea salt and pepper
1 1/2 C. chicken stock
1/4 C. white wine
four 4 oz. cod fillets

In a large skillet, heat olive oil over medium heat. Add garlic and sauté 1-2 minutes. Add spinach and let cook 1-2 minutes until just wilted, tossing well as it cooks. Add 2 t. butter, salt and pepper. Remove from pan and set aside. In the same pan, add stock, white wine, remaining 1 t. butter and salt and pepper. Bring to boil, add cod seasoned with salt and pepper, and reduce heat to low. Let cook 10 minutes until cooked through and serve over spinach.

Serves 4.

Very simple to prepare. The spinach is also delicious on its own as a side dish.

## LEFTOVERS
### Asian Fish Biscuits

leftover Cod with Sautéed Spinach
approx. 1/4 C. red cabbage, sliced thinly
approx. 1 T. hoisin sauce
biscuits or steam buns

Warm biscuits. Smear hoisin on bottom half. Add warmed leftover Cod with Sautéed Spinach. Top with red cabbage and remaining half of biscuit or steam bun.

## LEFTOVERS
### Fish Tacos

leftover Cod with Sautéed Spinach
one soft tortilla or taco shell
approx. 1/3 C. corn
one mango, sliced
approx. 1/8 C. avocado, cubed (optional)
sour cream
salsa

Warm leftover Cod with Sautéed Spinach. Place in tortilla. Top with corn, mango, avocado, sour cream and salsa.

## Pasta with Sausage, Fennel and Tomatoes

**Ingredients**

1 lb. pasta, such as fusilli
one link of mild italian sausage, casing removed
2 garlic cloves, finely chopped
1/2 C. onion, chopped
1 fennel bulb, sliced
sea salt and pepper

one 14.5 oz. can diced tomatoes
3/4 C. chicken broth
1 t. butter
2 T. parmesan cheese, grated
2 T. basil, chopped

Prepare pasta according to directions and drain. Meanwhile, add sausage broken into pieces to a large skillet over medium heat. Let cook 1 minute and add onion and garlic. Sauté 2 minutes. Add fennel and let cook 5 minutes until tender. Season with salt and pepper. Add can of diced tomatoes, broth and butter, and bring to simmer. Add pasta to pan and let cook 2-3 minutes to incorporate flavors. Add parmesan cheese and basil.

Serves 6.

Fennel and sausage are great together. Add additional vegetables, such as spinach or broccoli, if you prefer.

**5 minute dinner? Yep.**

## Sweet and Simple Pork Cutlets

**Ingredients**

1 lb. pork cutlets
1/8 t. garlic powder
sea salt and pepper
1 t. olive oil

1 T. apricot preserves
1/4 C. red wine
1 T. basil, chopped (optional)

Season pork cutlets with garlic powder, salt and pepper. Heat olive oil in a large skillet over medium to medium-high heat. Place cutlets in pan and cook 1-2 minutes, flip, and cook for an additional minute. Meanwhile, in a small bowl, whisk together apricot preserves with red wine. Add to pan with pork and let cook until reduced, for approximately 1-2 minutes. Cutlets will caramelize slightly. If sauce evaporates too much, add a drop of water. Top with basil, if preferred.

Serves 4.

Pork cutlets are just thin pork chops, and they cook super fast. The basil adds a nice pop of flavor but is not required. They still taste great without it.

# Roasted Chicken with Apples and Celery

**Ingredients**

four chicken breasts, bone-in with skin
sea salt and pepper
1 C. orange juice
four cloves of garlic, finely chopped

one apple, cored and thickly sliced
four celery stalks, cut into thirds
2 T. honey

Preheat oven to 425 degrees. Heat a large oven-safe skillet over medium heat. Pat chicken dry with paper towel, and season each piece with salt and pepper. Add two pieces to the pan skin-side down. Cook 4-5 minutes until browned, turn, and cook for an additional 4-5 minutes. Remove from pan and repeat with remaining chicken breasts. Add all chicken back to pan. Add juice over chicken and then rub garlic generously over top. Add apples and celery to pan. Drizzle honey over top of everything. Cook for 20-25 minutes in the oven until chicken is cooked through. Check on the chicken midway through cooking. If the orange juice has evaporated, add a drop of water.

Serves 4.

A delicious way to enjoy chicken.
Although roasting the breasts takes a little time, the recipe is fairly effortless.

## LEFTOVERS
### BBQ Chicken and Apple Pizza

2 tortillas
cooking spray
one leftover Roasted Chicken Breast with Apples and Celery (skin removed), meat coarsely pulled from bone
1/4 C. barbecue sauce
1/4 C. cheddar cheese, shredded
1 T. blue cheese, crumbled

Heat broiler.  Spray both sides of each tortilla with cooking spray.  Place on rack and let cook 1 minute.  Pop any bubbles and put browned-side down on a baking sheet.  Finely chop apples and celery, place in a small bowl, and combine with chicken and 2 T. BBQ sauce.  Put half of mixture over each tortilla.  Drizzle each tortilla with an additional 1 T. BBQ sauce, roughly spreading it around, and top each with half of both cheeses.  Broil 1-2 minutes.

## LEFTOVERS
### Apple Walnut Chicken Salad

one leftover Roasted Chicken Breast with Apples and Celery (skin removed)
1 T. onion, finely chopped
1 T. walnuts, chopped
1 T. raisins
1 T. plus 1 t. mayo
sea salt and pepper

Pull chicken off of the bone and shred finely with fingers.  Place in bowl.  Chop apples and celery, and add to bowl.  Add onion, walnuts, raisins and mayo, and toss to combine.  Season with salt and pepper to taste.

Here's to an apple a day...

## Turkey Burgers with Brie and Sauteed Apples

**Ingredients**

2 t. olive oil
two apples, such as fuji, thinly sliced
1/2 C. red onion, thinly sliced
1 lb. ground turkey
sea salt and pepper
1 t. rosemary, finely chopped

4 oz. brie, cut into 8 slices
3 T. light mayo
3/4 t. dijon mustard
3 T. honey
four english muffins

Heat olive oil in large non-stick skillet over medium heat. Add apples and onions and sauté approximately 3 minutes until golden and softened. Remove from heat and set aside. Meanwhile, in a medium bowl, combine turkey, salt, pepper and rosemary. Form into four patties and add to skillet. Cook 6-7 minutes, flip, and cook for an additional 6 minutes. Add two slices of Brie to each burger and let cook 2 minutes until melted. Toast English muffins. Add burger to bottom half of muffin, and top with sautéed apples and onions. In a small bowl, combine mayo, mustard and honey. Smear a quarter on the inside of the top half of muffin and cover burger.

Serves 4.

This can also be made with ground chicken (preferably not white meat).

# Seared Scallops with Cabbage

**Ingredients**

1 T. plus 1 t. olive oil
6 C. cabbage, chopped
sea salt and pepper

twelve sea scallops
1/2 C. red grapes, halved

Heat 1 t. olive oil in a large non-stick skillet over medium heat. Add cabbage, salt and pepper. Cover and let cook 10 minutes, stir, and let cook an additional 8-10 minutes until tender. Remove from pan and set aside. Add 1 1/2 t. olive oil to the skillet. Season both sides of scallops with salt and pepper. Place 6 scallops in the pan and cook for 2 minutes. Gently turn and cook for an additional 1-2 minutes until browned. Add cooked scallops to the plate with cabbage. Repeat the process with the remaining 6 scallops. Top the plate with grapes.

Serves 4.

The grapes add a burst of fresh flavor and color to the dish. As an alternative, use pomegranate seeds instead of grapes.

# Crispy Pan-Seared Salmon

**Ingredients**

four 4 oz. salmon fillets, skin removed
sea salt and pepper
2 t. dijon mustard
1 T. plus 1 t. honey

1/4 C. panko breadcrumbs
1 T. olive oil
one meyer or regular lemon

Season salmon fillets with salt and pepper and set aside. In a small bowl, combine mustard and honey, and blend well. Distribute honey mustard equally over each piece of salmon, spreading over top. Add 1 T. breadcrumbs to each, pressing down gently with your fingers so the breadcrumbs stick. Heat olive oil in a non-stick skillet over medium heat and add the salmon, breadcrumb-side down. Cook for 3-4 minutes until browned. Do not move fillets. Reduce heat slightly, and let cook for approximately 8 minutes or until cooked to desired doneness. Serve with lemon.

Serves 4.

This is a great way to prepare salmon – versatile and easy.

## LEFTOVERS
### Salmon and Cabbage Salad

one leftover Crispy Pan-Seared Salmon fillet
2 C. cabbage, thinly sliced
1 T. plus 1 t. peanut butter
1 T. orange juice
1 1/2 t. soy sauce
2 T. water
1/2 t. olive oil

In a medium bowl, gently break up the salmon fillet with a fork. Add cabbage. Set aside. In a small bowl, whisk together peanut butter with next four ingredients. Pour over top of salmon and cabbage, and toss to combine.

## LEFTOVERS  Salmon Cakes

one leftover Crispy Pan-Seared Salmon fillet
2 T. light mayo
1/4 t. dijon mustard
2 T. red pepper, chopped
one green onion or 1 T. red onion, chopped
cooking spray

Preheat broiler. In a medium bowl, break up salmon coarsely with a fork. Add mayo and next 3 ingredients. Prepare baking sheet with cooking spray. Divide salmon mixture into two heaping mounds on sheet, and press the mixture together with hands to form a patty shape. Place under broiler for 5-6 minutes.

# Working It™

## fast & fabulous: sides

- 34   Greek Cabbage Salad with Feta Toast
- 35   Zucchini with Corn and Tomatoes
- 36   Parmesan-Crusted Eggplant
- 37   *Make It a Meal:* Warm Romaine and Eggplant Salad
- 37   *Make It a Meal:* Eggplant and Bean Sandwiches
- 38   Quinoa with Nectarines and Arugula
- 39   Honeyed Green Beans
- 40   Creamy Cauliflower with Sage
- 41   *Make It a Meal:* Creamy Cauliflower Pasta
- 41   *Make It a Meal:* Cauliflower Soup
- 42   Couscous with Pistachios and Grapes
- 43   Roasted Baby Carrots with Basil
- 44   Roasted Brussels Sprouts with Chili Maple
- 45   Citrus Kale Salad
- 46   Watermelon Salad
- 47   *Make It a Meal:* Tuna with Watermelon and Mango Salad
- 47   *Make it a Meal:* Prosciutto, Cheese & Watermelon
- 50   Salad with Strawberries, Avocado and Peanuts
- 51   Sautéed Kale with Pumpkin Seeds
- 52   Roasted Sunflower Asparagus
- 53   *Make It a Meal:* Asparagus, Tomato and Sunflower Pasta
- 53   *Make It a Meal:* Asparagus, Egg & Brie
- 54   Potatoes with Sausage and Peppers
- 55   Country Salad
- 56   Roasted Tomatoes with Pine Nuts & Blue Cheese
- 57   *Make It a Meal:* Tomato, Roast Beef and Arugula Sandwiches
- 57   *Make It a Meal:* Chard, Beans and Tomatoes
- 58   Eggplant Roll-Ups
- 59   Roasted Cauliflower with Cranberries

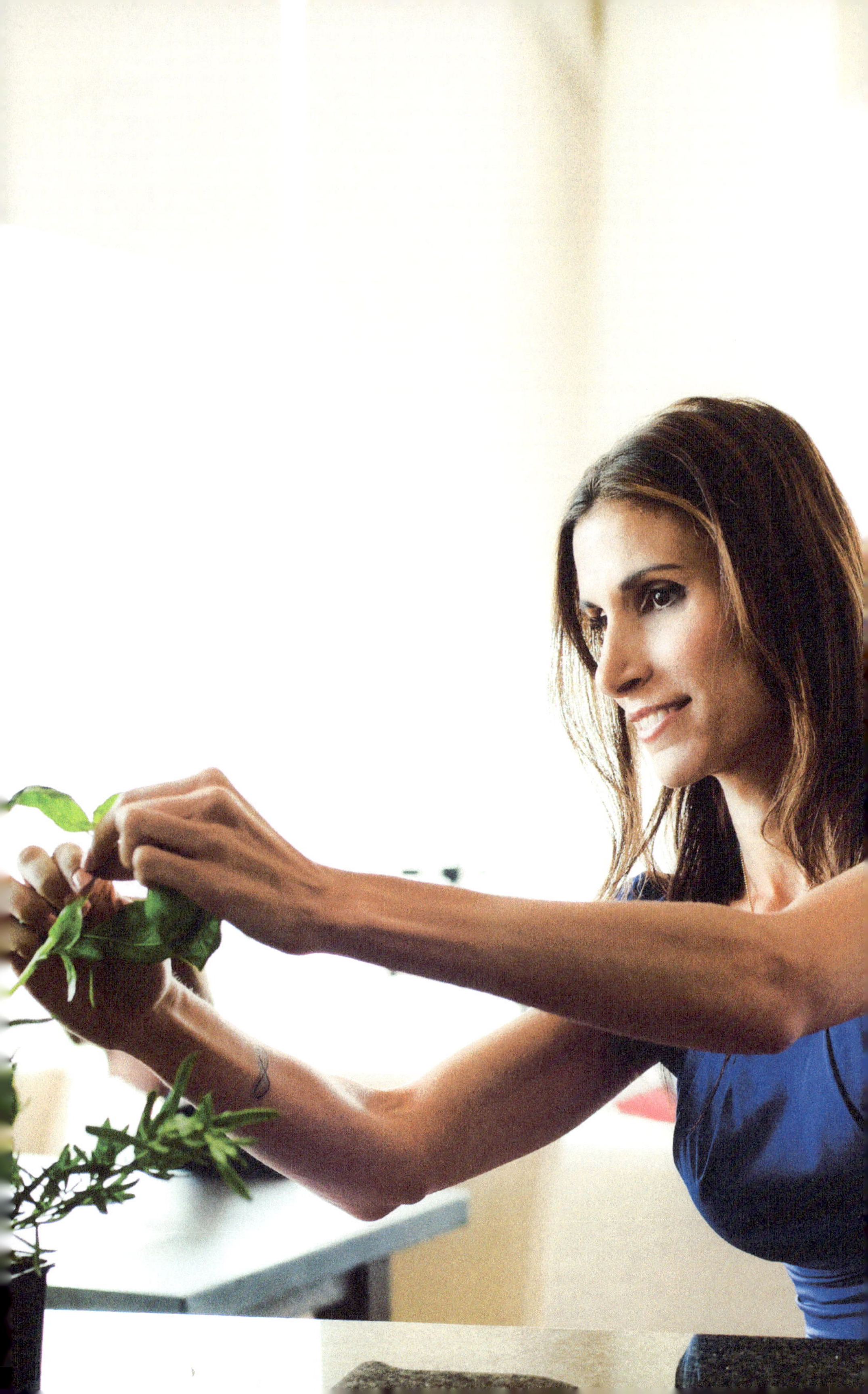

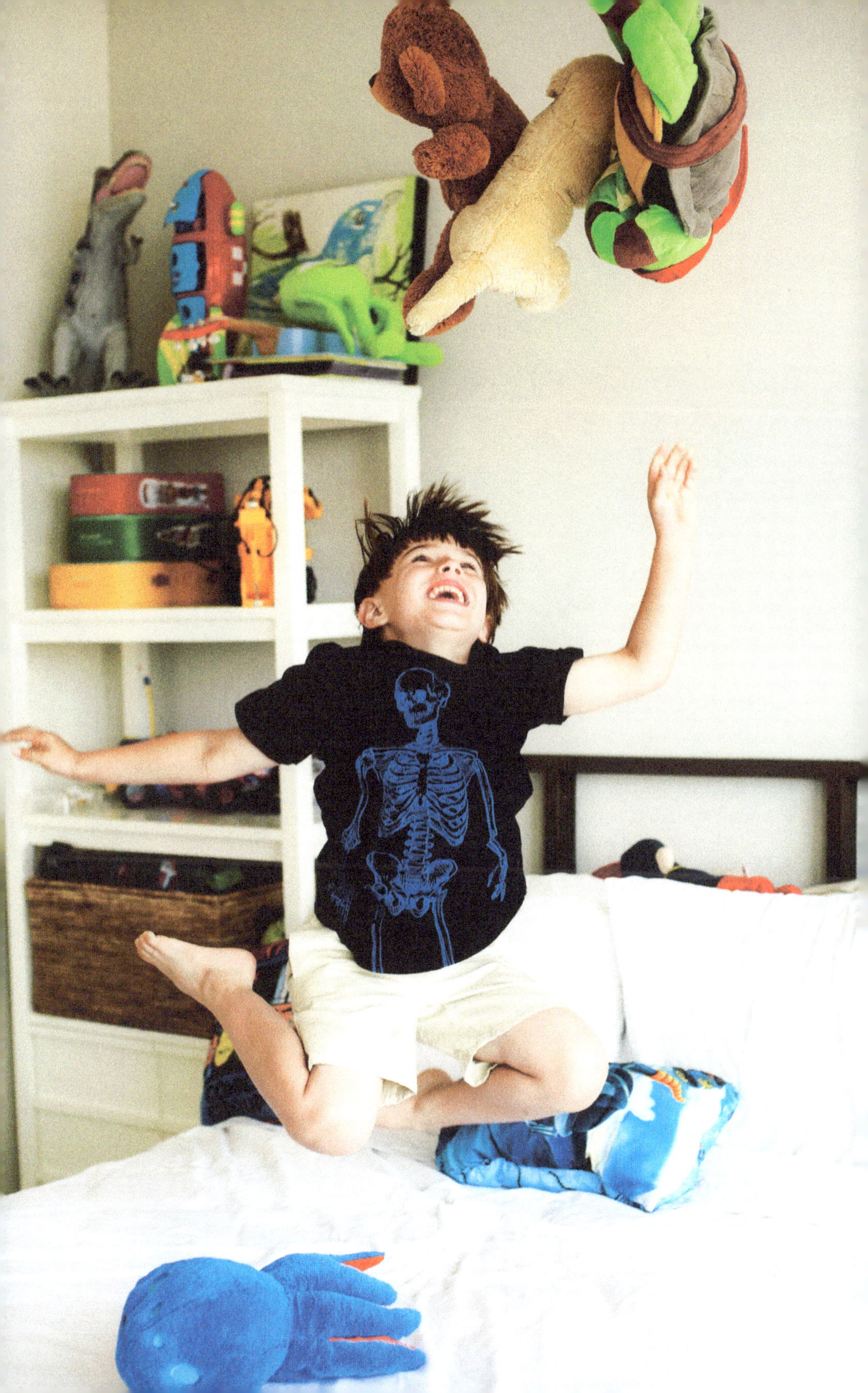

# Greek Cabbage Salad with Feta Toast

**Ingredients**

half a head of cabbage, sliced and chopped
1 C. grape tomatoes, halved
1/2 C. red onion, chopped
1/2 C. olives, halved
3 oz. feta cheese, crumbled
1/4 C. balsamic vinaigrette
sea salt and pepper

Feta Toast:
eight 1/4" slices of baguette
cooking spray
1/4 t. garlic powder
1 oz. feta cheese, crumbled

In a large bowl, combine cabbage with next 5 ingredients. Toss to combine. Season with salt and pepper to taste. Preheat broiler. Spray both sides of baguette slices with cooking spray and place on a baking sheet. Sprinkle each evenly with garlic powder and Feta crumbles. Place in oven for 2 minutes until just beginning to brown. Serve with salad.

Serves 4-6.

You can add kale to the salad as well for texture variation.

Summer year-round.

## Zucchini with Corn and Tomatoes

**Ingredients**

two zucchini squash, thinly sliced lengthwise
2 corn cobs, silk and husks removed
one red onion, thinly sliced

1 T. olive oil
sea salt and pepper
1 C. grape tomatoes, halved

Preheat broiler. Place zucchini over 3/4 of the length of a baking sheet. Place corn cobs on remaining 1/4 of sheet. Add onion slices over top of zucchini. Drizzle with olive oil and use your fingers to spread it around over everything. Season with salt and pepper. Cook for 5-6 minutes and remove from oven. Flip zucchini and onions with spatula and rotate corn. Cook for an additional 4-5 minutes until vegetables are tender and lightly brown on edges. If your broiler is extremely hot, cover with foil midway through cooking. Remove from oven and add tomatoes. Season with additional salt and pepper and cook for 1 minute. Remove from oven. Carefully cut kernels from corn cobs and toss together.

Serves 4-6.

This is a beautiful dish and effortless to make.

**Vegetables just got promoted.**

## Parmesan-Crusted Eggplant

**Ingredients**

one eggplant, ends removed
sea salt and pepper
cooking spray

1/8 t. garlic powder
1 C. parmesan cheese, grated

Slice eggplant with skin width-wise into 1/4" thick slices. Place in a large bowl filled with cool water and 1 t. salt, and let soak for 10 minutes. This extracts bitterness from the eggplant but will not make it salty. Drain, rinse and pat dry. Preheat oven to 400 degrees. Prepare baking sheet with cooking spray. Add eggplant. Spray eggplant with cooking spray and sprinkle with salt, pepper and garlic powder. Cook for approximately 10 minutes until eggplant is slightly tender. Remove from oven and flip eggplant. Spray top of eggplant with cooking spray and return to oven for 5 minutes. Remove from oven and switch oven to broil. Top each slice of eggplant generously with parmesan cheese, and return to oven for an additional 3-4 minutes until golden brown.

Serves 4-6.

> This is a regular dish in my house. Even my young son likes it.
> It's also great for lunch the next day.

## MAKE IT A MEAL   Warm Romaine and Eggplant Salad

Follow recipe for Parmesan-Crusted Eggplant
3 heads of romaine hearts, leaves washed and patted dry
1 T. olive oil
sea salt and pepper
1/4 C. raisins

Place romaine leaves on a baking sheet, drizzle with olive oil, and toss. Season with salt and pepper. Place in oven, heated to broil, for approximately 2 minutes until leaves are wilted and lightly browned around edges. Cut eggplant into quarters and place over top of romaine. Add raisins. Serves 4.

## MAKE IT A MEAL   Eggplant and Bean Sandwiches

Follow recipe for Parmesan-Crusted Eggplant
4 slices of good-quality bread
1 C. canned cannellini beans, drained and lightly rinsed
sea salt and pepper
4 slices mozzarella

Toast bread slices. In a small bowl, smash beans with the back of a fork. Season with salt and pepper. Place a quarter of bean mixture on top of each slice of bread. Add eggplant. Top each with a slice of mozzarella, and broil for 1-2 minutes until cheese is melted and lightly browned. Serves 4.

*A perfect way to eat this perfect food.*

## Quinoa with Nectarines and Arugula

**Ingredients**

2 t. butter
2 nectarines, slightly ripened and diced
1 C. quinoa
2 C. chicken broth

1 C. arugula
juice of half a lemon
sea salt

Melt 1 t. butter in a medium saucepan over medium heat. Add nectarines and sauté 3-4 minutes. Remove from pan and set aside. Add quinoa, broth and remaining 1 t. butter to pan, and bring to boil. Cover and reduce to low heat. Cook for 12 minutes until liquid is mostly evaporated. Remove from heat. Add arugula and toss until wilted. Add nectarines back to saucepan and drizzle with lemon juice. Season with salt to taste.

Serves 4.

Quinoa is healthy on its own. Combined with fruit and arugula, this is a power dish. If nectarines are not in season, use pears or apples.

## Honeyed Green Beans

**Ingredients**

1 lb. green beans, ends trimmed
1 t. olive oil
sea salt and pepper

1/8 t. garlic powder
2 t. butter
2 t. honey

Boil water in a large pot. Add green beans and salt to water, cook for 2-3 minutes, and drain. Heat olive oil in a large skillet over medium-high heat, and add green beans, salt, pepper and garlic powder. Cook 5 minutes tossing occasionally. Add butter and honey, and cook for an additional minute.

Serves 4-6.

To trim ends quickly, line up a bunch of green beans and cut ends with a knife. Repeat in batches.

*This may elicit requests for seconds. Make extra.*

## Creamy Cauliflower with Sage

**Ingredients**

one head of cauliflower
2 T. butter
1 T. plus 1 t. flour
2 1/2 C. low-fat milk

sea salt and pepper
1/4 C. parmesan cheese, grated
four-six sage leaves

Remove leaves and stem of cauliflower, and cut into florets. Rinse and set aside. Melt butter in a large skillet over medium heat, then add flour and stir well to combine. Let cook 1 minute, and add milk, salt and pepper. Let cook 5 minutes to thicken. Add cauliflower and additional salt to pan, reduce heat to low, and cook covered for 10 minutes until cauliflower is tender, stirring periodically. Add parmesan to pan. Break sage into pieces with fingers and add to pan, stir, and cook 2-3 minutes.

Serves 5.

The sage adds a nice flavor to the dish, but you can also make it without it. You can substitute basil or rosemary for the sage as well.

## MAKE IT A MEAL  Creamy Cauliflower Pasta

Follow recipe for Creamy Cauliflower with Sage using only half a head of cauliflower and all of the other ingredients

1/2 lb. pasta, such as fusilli
pinch sea salt

Follow directions for Creamy Cauliflower with Sage but reduce cauliflower to a half head. Reserve other half of cauliflower for another use, such as Roasted Cauliflower with Cranberries on page 59.  Meanwhile, prepare pasta according to package instructions.  Once pasta is cooked, drain, and add it to the skillet with the cauliflower.  Let sit for 3-4 minutes over low heat to incorporate flavors.  Add additional sage, parmesan and salt for taste, if preferred.
Serves 4.

## MAKE IT A MEAL  Cauliflower Soup

Follow recipe for Creamy Cauliflower with Sage
1 t. olive oil
1/2 C. onion, chopped
6 C. chicken stock
1/4 C. cream or half-and-half

Heat oil in a large saucepan over medium heat.  Add onion and saute about 2 minutes until translucent.  Add prepared cauliflower mixture using a spatula to gather all of the sauce.  Break up any larger pieces of cauliflower with a fork or spoon. Add stock and let cook 10 minutes. Add cream and cook 2 minutes. Add additional sage, parmesan and salt to taste, if preferred.
Serves 5.

## Cous Cous with Pistachios and Grapes

**Ingredients**

1 2/3 C. chicken broth
1 T. butter
sea salt

1 C. couscous
1/2 C. pistachio nuts, shelled
1 C. grapes, halved

In a small saucepan, bring broth to boil. Add couscous, butter and 1/2 t. salt. Cover and remove from heat. Let sit for 5 minutes until liquid is absorbed. Add pistachios and grapes, and combine together using a fork to fluff couscous.

Serves 4.

A simple weeknight dish that takes 10 minutes to prepare.

**Beta-carotene never tasted so good.**

# Roasted Baby Carrots with Basil

**Ingredients**

3 C. baby carrots
1. olive oil
1 T. butter

1/3 C. orange juice
1/4 C. basil, chopped
sea salt

Preheat oven to 400 degrees.  Place carrots in an 8"x 8" baking dish with olive oil, and toss to coat.  Add butter and place in oven for approximately 25 minutes.  Remove from oven, add juice, and return to oven for 8 additional minutes until juice is reduced and carrots are tender.  Do not burn; add more juice if needed.  Remove from oven, add basil, and season with salt to taste.

Serves 4.

A great way to use baby carrots, but you can also slice full-sized carrots. This dish takes a little while to cook, but prep is a breeze.

# Roasted Brussels Sprouts with Chili Maple

**Ingredients**

1 lb. brussels sprouts
1 T. olive oil
sea salt

2 t. maple syrup
1/8 t. chili powder

Preheat oven to 400 degrees. Trim ends of brussels sprouts and cut each in half. Place on a baking sheet. Add olive oil and salt, and toss well to combine. Cook for 10 minutes, remove from oven, toss, and return to oven for an additional 5 minutes. Remove from oven, drizzle with maple syrup, and sprinkle chili powder. Toss to combine.

Serves 4.

These taste great cold the next day mixed into a green salad.
Try them combined with pecans and blue cheese.
If you find the sprouts to be too hard, par boil them next time before roasting.

## Citrus Kale Salad

**Ingredients**

one bunch of kale, center ribs and stems removed
two oranges
4 oz. blue cheese, crumbled

1/4 C. almonds, whole or chopped
1 T. olive oil
sea salt and pepper

Break kale leaves into pieces. Place in a large bowl and set aside. Cut the ends off of one orange. Place it flat on cutting board and cut away the peel. Cut the orange into segments, removing the membranes in between leaving only the flesh, then cut the segments into small pieces. Add oranges to the bowl with kale along with blue cheese and almonds. Cut the other orange in half and squeeze the juice of both halves over kale. Drizzle with olive oil and toss to combine. Season with salt and pepper.

Serves 4-6.

This dish is packed with powerful nutrients.
Feta can be used in place of blue cheese.

**A fruit salad remix.**

# Watermelon Salad

**Ingredients**

5 C. watermelon, cubed
2 T. basil, chopped

1 T. balsamic vinegar
sea salt (optional)

In a medium bowl, combine watermelon and basil. Drizzle with balsamic vinegar. Sprinkle with pinch of salt. Toss gently.

Serves 5.

Pair with a sharp cheese, such as Piave or provolone, and bread for a delicious snack or lunch. Other melons can also be added.

## MAKE IT A MEAL — Tuna with Watermelon and Mango Salad

Follow recipe for Watermelon Salad
one mango, cubed
4 tuna steaks

sea salt and pepper
1 t. olive oil
2 T. balsamic vinegar

In a small bowl, combine 1 C. Watermelon Salad with mango. Reserve remaining Watermelon Salad for another use. Toss to combine and set aside. Season tuna with salt and pepper. Heat olive oil in a large skillet over medium heat. Add tuna and cook for 3-4 minutes. Flip and cook for an additional 3-4 minutes or until cooked to desired doneness. Top each piece of fish evenly with watermelon and mango salad.
Serves 4.

## MAKE IT A MEAL — Prosciutto, Cheese & Watermelon

Follow recipe for Watermelon Salad
4 slices of wheat bread, toasted
8 slices of prosciutto
4 oz. mozzarella
basil leaves

Preheat broiler. Place two slices of prosciutto on top of each slice of toast. Add 1 oz. mozzarella to each, and place under broiler for 1-2 minutes until cheese is melted. Remove from oven. Add a few leaves of basil to each slice of bread, and top with 1/4 C. of Watermelon Salad. Reserve remaining Watermelon Salad for another use.
Serves 4.

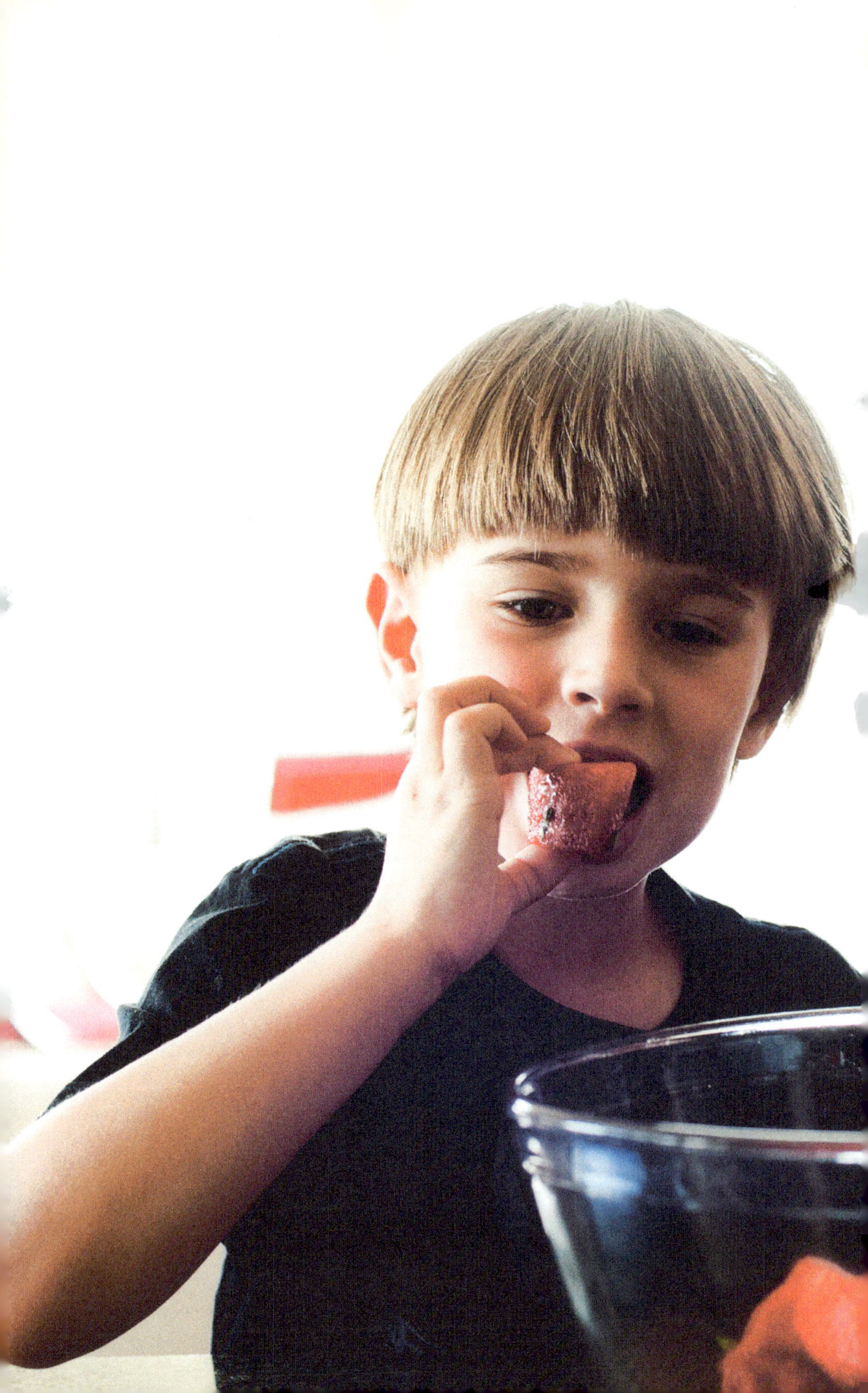

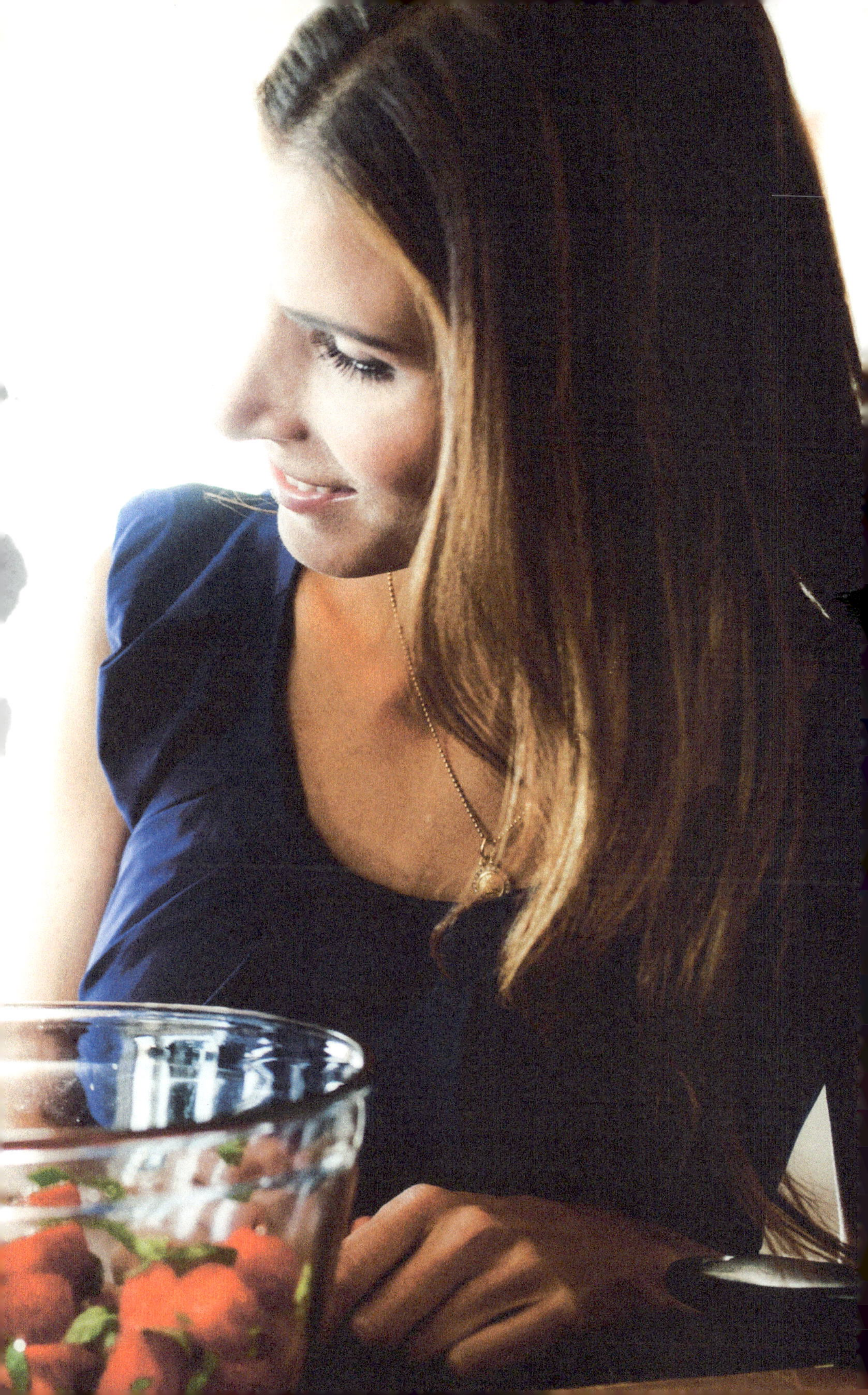

## Salad with Strawberries, Avocado and Peanuts

**Ingredients**

6 C. lettuce, such as bibb, romaine or red leaf, washed, dried and broken into pieces
one quart strawberries, sliced
3/4 C. avocado, cubed

1/2 C. good-quality peanuts
one lemon
1 T. olive oil
sea salt and pepper

Place lettuce in a large bowl. Add strawberries, avocado and peanuts. Squeeze lemon over top and drizzle with olive oil. Toss to combine. Season with salt and pepper to taste.

Serves 4.

With salted peanuts, you won't need to add much extra.
Using good-quality peanuts is important.

# Sautéed Kale with Pumpkin Seeds

**Ingredients**

**1 1/2 t. olive oil**
**one bunch of kale, ribs and stems removed and leaves broken coarsely into thirds**

**sea salt and pepper**
**3 T. pumpkin (pepita) seeds**

Heat olive oil in a large skillet over medium heat. Add kale leaves, tossing regularly for approximately 5 minutes until leaves are wilted. Season with salt and pepper. Add pumpkin seeds and toss to combine.

Serves 4-6.

This is a very simple preparation, and the seeds add great crunch.

## Roasted Sunflower Asparagus

**Ingredients**

1 lb. asparagus, ends trimmed
1 T. olive oil
sea salt and pepper

1/4 C. sunflower seeds, shelled
1/4 C. parmesan cheese, grated

Preheat oven to 400 degrees. Add asparagus and olive oil to baking sheet and toss to combine. Sprinkle with salt and pepper, and place in oven for approximately 8-10 minutes or until tender. Cook time depends on thickness of asparagus spears. Remove from oven, add sunflower seeds, and then parmesan cheese generously over top. Place back in oven for 2-3 minutes until cheese is melted.

Serves 6.

The sunflower seeds add great crunch as well as protein.

## MAKE IT A MEAL
### Asparagus, Tomato and Sunflower Pasta

Follow recipe for Roasted Sunflower Asparagus
1 1/2 C. grape tomatoes, halved
1 lb. pasta, such as linguini
1/8 C. parmesan cheese
sea salt and pepper

Follow directions for Roasted Sunflower Asparagus, but right before adding the sunflower seeds and parmesan cheese, add tomatoes to the pan and then follow remaining instructions. Transfer to a large bowl. Meanwhile, prepare pasta according to package instructions. Once pasta is cooked, drain, reserving 1/2 C. cooking liquid. Add the pasta and cooking liquid to the bowl with the asparagus and tomatoes. Toss to combine. Season with salt and pepper. Serves 6.

## MAKE IT A MEAL   Asparagus, Egg and Brie

Follow recipe for Roasted Sunflower Asparagus, halving all measurements
4 slices of wheat bread, toasted
4 oz. brie, sliced
1 t. butter
4 eggs
sea salt

Prepare half of asparagus recipe and set aside. Add 1 oz. Brie to each slice of toast and place in oven to melt. Meanwhile, in large skillet over medium heat, melt 1/2 t. butter. Crack two eggs into pan, keeping them apart. Sprinkle with salt and cook 1-2 minutes. Gently flip and cook 20 seconds. Remove from pan and repeat with last eggs. Place eggs onto toast with melted cheese. Top with asparagus spears. Serves 4.

My version of country cooking.

## Potatoes with Sausage and Peppers

**Ingredients**

one link mild italian sausage, casing removed
4 potatoes, such as yukon gold, diced
1 red pepper, chopped

one garlic clove, chopped
1 C. chicken broth

Break sausage into small pieces and heat in large skillet over medium heat for 1-2 minutes.  Add potatoes, peppers and garlic.  Sauté 10-12 minutes until browned.  Add broth and cover.  Let cook an additional 8-10 minutes until potatoes are tender.

Serves 5.

The sausage gives this dish amazing flavor.

**Salad minus the lettuce.**

# Country Salad

**Ingredients**

two medium tomatoes, stems removed
one english cucumber, thinly sliced and halved
half a red pepper, thinly sliced
half a small red onion, thinly sliced

one green onion, chopped
1/4 C. light sour cream
3 T. parsley, chopped
sea salt

Cut tomato in half end-to-end. Cut each half into quarters and place in a large bowl. Add next 6 ingredients. Season generously with salt. Toss well to combine.

Serves 4-6.

This salad tastes best after sitting for a few hours once the juices come together. Dip bread into the juice. Cilantro can be used instead of parsley.

*Fruit or vegetable? Who cares.*

## Roasted Tomatoes with Pine Nuts & Blue Cheese

**Ingredients**

four roma tomatoes
cooking spray
sea salt and pepper

1 T. plus 1 t. blue cheese, crumbled
2 t. pine nuts
1 1/2 t. olive oil

Preheat broiler. Cut both ends off tomatoes and slice in half widthwise. Place on a baking sheet coated with cooking spray. Sprinkle lightly with salt and pepper. Place 1/2 t. blue cheese on top of each tomato half, then add 1/4 t. pine nuts to each. Drizzle each lightly with olive oil and cook for approximately 8-10 minutes until tender.

Serves 4.

A very versatile dish.
Layer the tomatoes on crusty Italian bread for an alternative to a mozzarella and tomato sandwich, or eat with scrambled eggs and salad greens.

## MAKE IT A MEAL
### Tomato, Roast Beef and Arugula Sandwiches

Follow recipe for Roasted Tomatoes with Pine Nuts & Blue Cheese, halving all measurements
two pitas, cut in half
2 T. light mayo
1/4 t. dijon mustard
1/2 lb. roast beef, thinly sliced
1/2 C. arugula

Warm pitas. In small bowl, combine mayo and mustard. Spread mixture on the inside bottom of pita. Layer roast beef, then arugula. Cut tomatoes in half so not as thick, and layer in sandwich. Serves 2.

## MAKE IT A MEAL   Chard, Beans and Tomatoes

Follow recipe for Roasted Tomatoes with Pine Nuts & Blue Cheese
1 bunch chard, ends and ribs cut from leaves; reserve all
1 t. olive oil
2 cloves garlic, chopped
sea salt and pepper
one 15.5 oz. can cannellini beans, lightly rinsed and drained

Heat olive oil in pan over medium heat. Add garlic and saute 1 minute. Add ribs and stems of chard, cut into thirds, to pan, season with salt and pepper, and saute 8 minutes till tender. Chop chard leaves into thirds and add to pan with beans. Season with salt and pepper and cook 4 minutes. Serve with tomatoes. Serves 3.

**So simple. So good.**

# Eggplant Roll-Ups

**Ingredients**

one eggplant, ends removed
sea salt and pepper
1 T. olive oil

1/4 C. light sour cream
1 small garlic clove, crushed
1/8 C. tomatoes, diced

Slice eggplant with skin lengthwise into 1/8" thick slices. Place in a large bowl filled with cool water and 1 t. salt, and let soak for 10 minutes. This extracts bitterness from the eggplant but will not make it salty. Drain, rinse and pat dry. Preheat oven to 400 degrees. Add eggplant slices to pan and brush both sides with olive oil. Sprinkle with salt and pepper. Cook for approximately 10 minutes until eggplant is slightly tender. Remove from oven, flip, and return to oven for 5 minutes. In a small bowl, combine sour cream, garlic, salt and pepper. Place a dollop of the sour cream mixture at one end of each slice of eggplant. Add tomatoes evenly over each dollop of sour cream. Roll up eggplant beginning at the filled end.

Serves 6.

Try the eggplant with something other than tomatoes for variety - sauteed spinach would be delicious.

# Roasted Cauliflower with Cranberries

**Ingredients**

one head of cauliflower, cut into florets
3 T. olive oil

sea salt and pepper
1 C. dried cranberries

Preheat oven to 400 degrees. Place cauliflower on a baking sheet. Add olive oil, salt and pepper, and toss well to combine. Place in oven and cook for approximately 10 minutes. Remove from heat and toss lightly. Return to oven and cook for an additional 8-10 minutes until lightly golden and tender. Remove from oven, add cranberries, and toss to combine.

Serves 6.

This is an absolutely beautiful side dish.
Elegant enough to serve for a holiday, but easy enough for a weeknight.

# Working It™

## pantry dive™

66  Egg Soufflés
67  Fried Eggs with Potatoes and Peppers
68  Ricotta Flatbread Pizza
69  Olive, Feta & Chickpea Flatbread Pizza
70  Beans with Sautéed Potatoes
71  Peas and Pasta
72  Ricotta Pasta
73  Roasted Pepper Pasta with Walnuts
74  Tuna with Olives over Rice
75  Tuna with Potatoes and Capers
76  Cheddar Corn Chowder
77  Stracciatella
78  Broccoli and Roasted Pepper Paninis
79  Spinach Artichoke Paninis
80  Mozzarella Cutlets
81  Rice Balls with Artichokes & Mozzarella

# PANTRY DIVE™ GUIDE

## A Well-Stocked Pantry

Nothing to eat in the house? No plan for dinner?

Keeping a well-stocked pantry can transform cereal night into a proper meal. Here is a list of suggestions on what to keep on-hand and recipes to help you use them.

- Milk, cream or half-and-half, and orange juice

- Pasta, rice, breadcrumbs and tortillas

- Olive oil, honey, maple syrup, mayo, Dijon mustard, ketchup, BBQ sauce, balsamic vinegar, tomato paste, apricot preserves, salsa, sour cream and chicken stock

- Ricotta, parmesan, and at least one other cheese. Rotate them to give you variety and options. I suggest one that is good for melting, such as fontina, cheddar, mozzarella, gruyere, manchego, etc. And one with bite, such as feta or blue cheese

- Canned goods including corn, a few types of beans – such as black, cannellini and garbanzo – olives, diced tomatoes, roasted peppers, tuna, capers and artichoke hearts

- Two types of nuts, such as almonds or walnuts

- Fresh perishable foods that last relatively long: apples or pears, potatoes (white and/or sweet), lemons, oranges, eggs, avocados, peppers, garlic and onions

- Frozen foods, such as peas, broccoli, spinach and a leftover baguette loaf

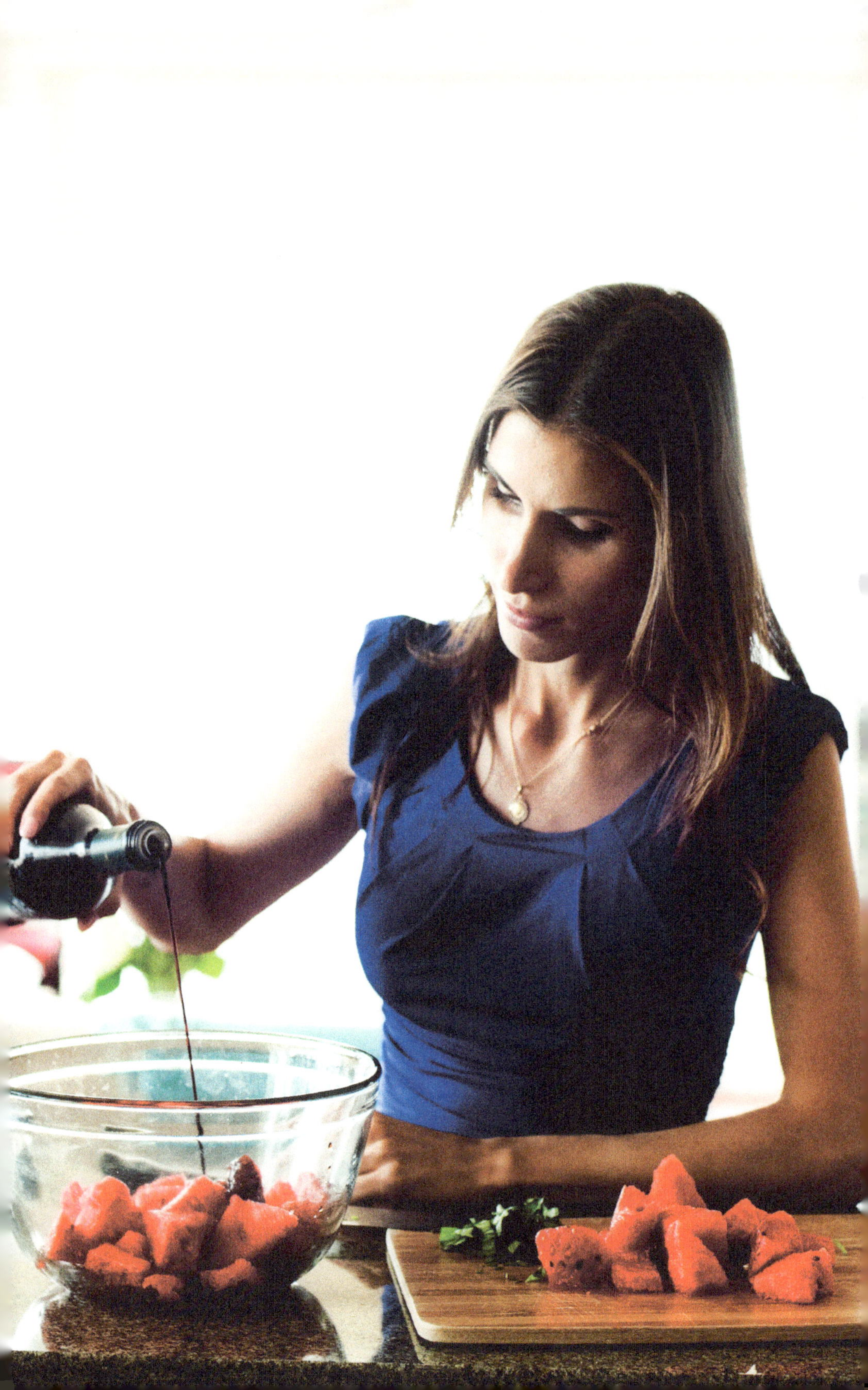

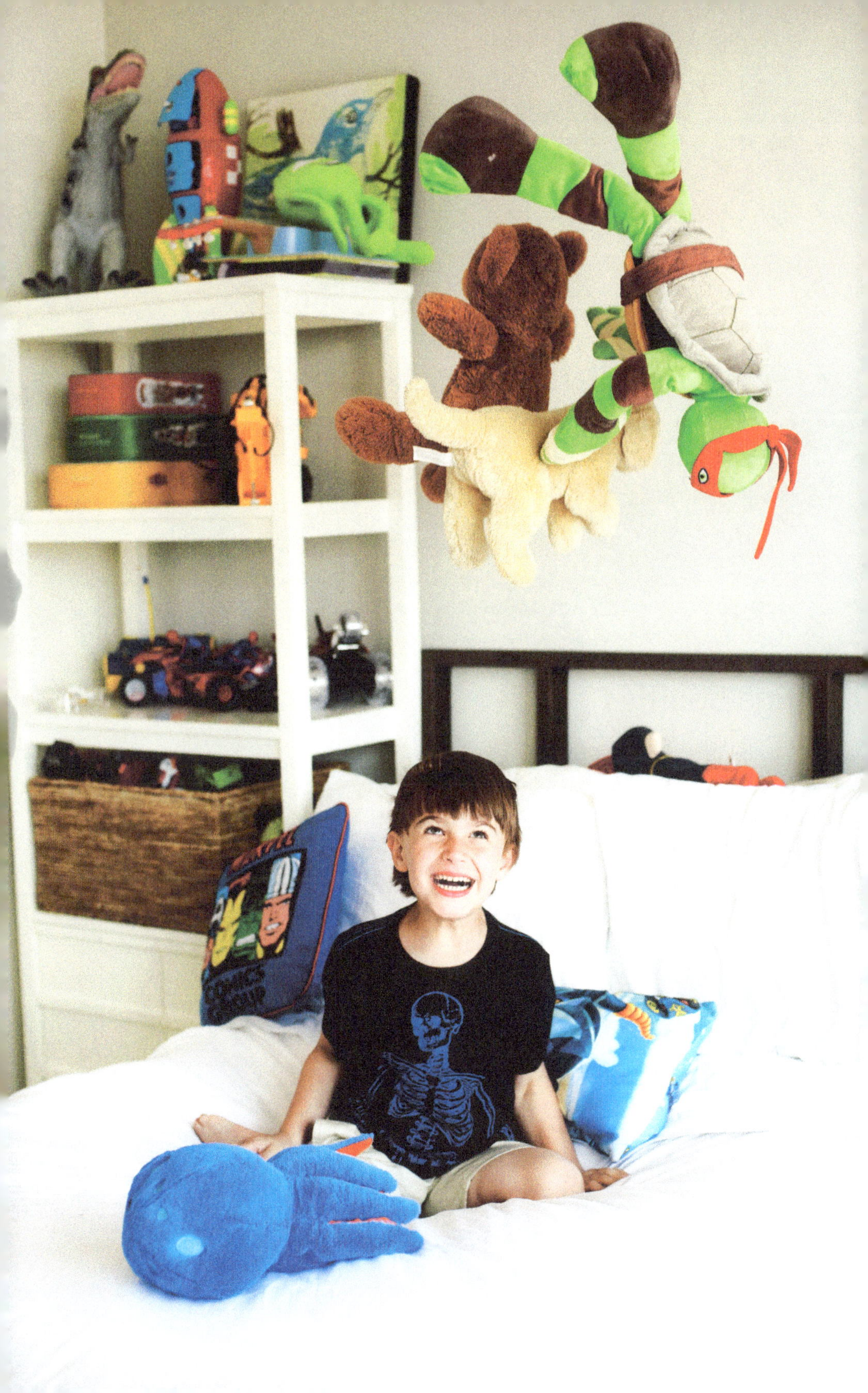

**Stale bread reinvented.**

## Egg Soufflés

**Ingredients**

cooking spray
half a loaf of stale baguette
four eggs

1 C. milk
sea salt and pepper
1/2 C. gruyere cheese, grated

Preheat oven to 350 degrees. Spray a cupcake pan with cooking spray. Set aside. Cut stale bread into 1/2" cubes. Place about 1/3 C. of bread cubes into six cupcake holders. In a small bowl, whisk egg, milk, salt and pepper. Add egg mixture evenly over bread in each holder. Top each one with 1 T. plus 1 t. of the cheese. Place in oven and let cook 20-25 minutes.

Serves 6.

Substitute another cheese that you prefer or have on-hand.
You can use fresh bread, but bake it in the oven once it's cut into cubes to crispen it.

## Fried Eggs with Potatoes and Peppers

**Ingredients**

1 T. olive oil
one red pepper, sliced thin
half a small red onion
two large potatoes, such as yukon gold

sea salt
1/8 t. garlic powder
two eggs

Preheat broiler. Heat 1 t. olive oil in large ovenproof skillet over medium heat. Add red pepper and sauté 2-3 minutes. Add onion and sauté 1-2 minutes until slightly softened. Slice potatoes into very thin circles and add to pan. Add remaining 2. t. olive oil and salt. Toss and using a spoon, push potatoes so they are flat, covering the bottom of pan. Transfer pan to broiler for 10 minutes until potatoes are soft and golden brown. If your broiler is extremely hot, cover the potatoes with foil midway through cooking so they don't burn. Remove from oven carefully and transfer to plate. Place skillet back on stovetop and crack two eggs into it, keeping them separate. Sprinkle lightly with salt and cook 1-2 minutes. Gently flip, and cook an additional 20 seconds.

Serves 2.

If you don't have a fresh pepper on-hand, use 1/3 C. jarred roasted red peppers, but add them after the onion.
Be careful with the handle of the pan when transferring from broiler to stovetop.

**Simple. Fast. Delicious.**

## Ricotta Flatbread Pizza

**Ingredients**

four tortillas
cooking spray
2 T. olive oil
1/2 C. ricotta

sea salt
1/2 C. fontina cheese, grated
1/4 C. parmesan cheese, grated
1/2 t. red pepper flakes

Preheat broiler. Spray both sides of each tortilla with cooking spray, and place under broiler directly on the rack for approximately 2 minutes until crisp on top. Remove from oven and, with a fork, pop any large bubbles that have formed. Turn the tortillas crisp-side down and drizzle 1 t. olive oil over the top of each. Add 2 T. of ricotta onto each tortilla in small dollops and sprinkle with salt. Add 2 T. of fontina and 1 T. parmesan over top of each. Drizzle each with an additional 1/2 t. olive oil and sprinkle with 1/8 t. red pepper flakes. Place back under broiler for 1-2 minutes until melted and golden brown.

Serves 4.

> Substitute another cheese that you prefer or have on-hand. Tortillas are a versatile and fast option for weekdays.

## Olive, Feta & Chickpea Flatbread Pizza

**Ingredients**

four tortillas
cooking spray
1/2 C. roasted red peppers, chopped
1/2 C. canned chickpeas, rinsed and drained

1/2 C. olives, chopped
1 C. cheddar cheese, grated
1/2 C. feta cheese, crumbled

Preheat broiler. Spray both sides of each tortilla with cooking spray, and place under broiler directly on the rack for approximately 2 minutes until crisp on top. Remove from the oven and, with a fork, pop any large bubbles that have formed. Turn the tortillas crisp-side down and add 2 T. roasted red peppers, 2 T. chickpeas and 2 T. olives to each. Add 1/4 C. cheddar cheese and 1/8 C. Feta cheese over top of each. Place back under broiler for 1-2 minutes until melted and golden brown.

Serves 4.

This is so good. Pantry items rock.

# Beans with Sautéed Potatoes

Ingredients

2 t. olive oil
three large potatoes, such as yukon gold, diced
sea salt
1/4 t. cumin
1/4 t. chili powder
1/4 t. garlic powder

one 15.5 oz. can black beans, lightly rinsed and lightly drained
1/3 C. cheese such as cheddar or fontina, shredded
1/4 C. salsa

Heat olive oil in a large non-stick skillet over medium-low heat. Add potatoes and salt, and cook for 12-15 minutes until lightly brown and tender. Add 1/8 t. each of cumin, chili powder and garlic powder. Sauté an additional 2-3 minutes. Add black beans, season with salt, and add remaining 1/8 t. of cumin, chili powder and garlic powder. Cook 1-2 minutes to incorporate flavors and remove from heat. Add cheese and let melt. Serve with salsa.

Serves 4.

> You can use most any bean that you have on-hand: black beans, white beans or pinto beans are all terrific options.

**Beans and rice have a newfound competitor.**

## Peas and Pasta

**Ingredients**

1 lb. pasta, such as orechiette
3 T. butter
1/3 C. almonds, coarsely chopped

2 C. frozen peas, unthawed
1/4 C. parmesan cheese, grated
sea salt and pepper

Prepare pasta according to directions and drain, reserving 2/3 C. cooking liquid. Meanwhile, melt butter in a large skillet over medium heat. Add almonds and sautè 1-2 minutes. Add frozen peas and let cook an additional 1-2 minutes. Add cooked pasta and reserved water to skillet. Let cook 2-3 minutes and top with parmesan cheese. Season with salt and pepper.

Serves 6.

The almonds add wonderful flavor and texture to this dish.
Walnuts would also be a fine substitute.

## Ricotta Pasta

**Ingredients**

1 lb. pasta, such as cavatappi, fusilli or ziti
2 T. butter
1/2 C. ricotta
1/4 C. parmesan cheese, grated
sea salt and pepper

Prepare pasta according to directions and drain, reserving 2/3 C. cooking liquid. Place pasta back into hot saucepan. Add butter and ricotta to hot pasta and toss to combine. Add parmesan cheese and reserved cooking liquid. Season with salt and pepper.

Serves 4.

I love easy-cleanup dinners!
With a no-cook sauce, this dish is a winner in both taste and convenience.

*Grandma would be proud.*

## Roasted Pepper Pasta with Walnuts

Ingredients

1 lb. pasta, such as spaghetti
2 T. butter
2 garlic cloves, finely chopped
pinch red pepper flakes
1 C. jarred roasted peppers, drained and finely chopped

2 C. broth
1/8 C. half-and-half
1/2 C. walnuts
sea salt and pepper
parmesan cheese

Prepare pasta according to directions and drain. Meanwhile, heat butter in large skillet over medium heat. Add garlic and red pepper flakes and sauté 1 minute. Add red peppers and broth, and bring to boil. Reduce heat and add half-and-half and walnuts. Let cook to incorporate flavors and reduce slightly for about 5 minutes. Add pasta to skillet and cook for an additional 5 minutes. Sprinkle with parmesan cheese to taste.

Serves 6.

Roasted peppers go from a condiment to a star ingredient in this dish.

## Tuna with Olives over Rice

**Ingredients**

white rice
1 t. olive oil
1/3 C. onion, finely chopped
2 T. tomato paste

1 C. chicken broth or stock
two 5 oz. cans tuna, drained
1/4 C. olives, chopped

Prepare rice according to package instructions. Meanwhile, heat olive oil in a large skillet over medium heat. Add onion and sauté 2 minutes. Add tomato paste and cook 1-2 minutes. Add broth and cook 4 minutes. Coarsely break up tuna with a fork and add to skillet. Cook for 1 minute. Remove from heat and add olives over top. Serve over rice.

Serves 4.

A warm tuna salad using a handful of ingredients.
This can also be served cold the next day with crackers in lieu of rice.

# Tuna with Potatoes and Capers

**Ingredients**

1 T. plus 1/2 t. olive oil
3 potatoes such as yukon gold, diced
sea salt and pepper
1/4 onion, chopped

two 5 oz. cans of tuna in water, drained
2 t. orange juice
3 T. capers, drained

Heat 1 1/2 t. olive oil in a large skillet over medium heat. Add potatoes to pan, season with salt and pepper, and sauté for about 12 minutes. Add onion and sauté an additional 4-5 minutes until potatoes and onion are tender and lightly golden. Meanwhile, in a small bowl, break up tuna coarsely with a fork. Add remaining 2 t. olive oil, orange juice and capers to tuna. Season with salt and pepper, and toss lightly. Serve tuna over potatoes.

Serves 4.

Simple, good and effortless. You can substitute lemon juice for the orange juice.

## Cheddar Corn Chowder

**Ingredients**

1 t. olive oil
1/4 C. red pepper, chopped
1/4 C. red onion, chopped
one medium potato, such as yukon gold, diced
one 15.5 oz. can of whole corn kernels

3/4 C. low-sodium chicken stock
one bay leaf
1/3 C. cream
sea salt and pepper
1/8 C. cheddar cheese, grated

Heat olive oil in a medium saucepan over medium heat. Add red pepper and onion, and sauté for 2-3 minutes. Add potatoes and let cook 2 minutes stirring often to avoid sticking. Add can of corn, including the liquid from the can (do not drain), chicken stock, bay leaf and cream. Bring to boil and reduce heat. Cook covered for approximately 15 minutes until potatoes are tender and soup is thickened. Season with salt and pepper to taste. Remove bay leaf. Add cheese over top of each bowl before serving.

Serves 2.

Add diced avocado, a dollop of sour cream and tortilla chips, if you have the items on-hand, to add additional flavor and texture.

*Homemade soup in minutes.*

## Stracciatella

**Ingredients**

8 C. chicken stock
2 eggs
1 t. parmesan cheese, grated
sea salt and pepper
1/2 C. frozen spinach, thawed and drained
1 C. pastina

Parmesan Crisps:
cooking spray
1/4 C. parmesan cheese, grated

Preheat broiler. Bring stock to boil in a medium saucepan. Reduce to simmer. In a small bowl, whisk together eggs, pinch of salt and pepper, and parmesan. Slowly drizzle eggs while stirring gently. Add frozen spinach and pastina. Stir gently and let cook 4-5 minutes until pasta is cooked. Meanwhile, coat baking sheet with cooking spray. Place four 1 T. mounds of parmesan cheese on the pan. Broil for 30-60 seconds until golden. Serve with soup.

Serves 4.

Fresh spinach is preferred if you have it on-hand.
This is also good with ravioli or tortellini.

**Broccoli sandwiches are underrated.**

## Broccoli and Roasted Pepper Paninis

**Ingredients**

eight slices of rustic wheat bread
2 C. frozen broccoli florets, thawed
2/3 C. cheddar cheese, shredded

2 T. roasted peppers, drained and chopped
2 T. light mayo
cooking spray

Preheat broiler. Place four slices of bread on baking sheet; reserve remaining four slices. In a small bowl, combine broccoli with next 3 ingredients. Top each slice of bread with a quarter of the mixture. Place remaining slices of bread on top and spray with cooking spray. Place under the broiler for 2-3 minutes. Remove from oven and flip. Spray again with cooking spray and return to the oven for an additional 2-3 minutes. If cheese is not fully melted, cover with foil and place back in oven for a few additional minutes.

Serves 4.

Substitute with another cheese that you prefer or have on-hand.

# Spinach Artichoke Paninis

**Ingredients**

eight slices of rustic wheat bread
one 9 oz. pkg frozen spinach, thawed and drained
1/8 t. garlic powder
sea salt and pepper

one 6 oz. jar marinated artichoke hearts, drained
1 C. mozzarella, shredded
1/4 C. light mayo
cooking spray

Preheat broiler. Place four slices of bread on baking sheet; reserve remaining four slices. In a small bowl, combine spinach with garlic powder, salt and pepper. Spread a quarter of spinach evenly over bread. Chop artichoke hearts and add over top. In a small bowl, combine mozzarella with mayo. Spread a quarter of the mixture on top of each. Place remaining slices of bread on top and spray with cooking spray. Place under the broiler for 2-3 minutes. Remove from oven and flip. Spray again with cooking spray and return to the oven for an additional 2-3 minutes. If cheese is not fully melted, cover with foil and place back in oven for a few additional minutes.

Serves 4.

A real crowd pleaser! Spinach never tasted so good.

**Cheese, please.**

## Mozzarella Cutlets

**Ingredients**

three eggs
2 C. panko breadcrumbs

one 16 oz. package mozzarella, cut into 8 slices
4 T. olive oil

In a small bowl, beat eggs and set aside. Place breadcrumbs in another small bowl and set aside. Dredge each mozzarella slice in egg, then breadcrumbs, then back in egg and once more in breadcrumbs, and set aside. Heat 2 T. olive oil in a large non-stick skillet over medium heat. Add 4 slices of prepared mozzarella. Cook 1 1/2 minutes, flip, and cook for an additional 1 1/2 minutes. Repeat with remaining four slices. Serve immediately.

Serves 4.

Dinner in less than 10 minutes! Adults and kids alike will eat every mouthful.

## Rice Balls with Artichokes & Mozzarella

**Ingredients**

2 1/2 C. prepared rice
1/4 C. ricotta
2 eggs
one 6 oz. jar marinated artichoke hearts, drained and chopped

sea salt and pepper
3/4 C. italian seasoned breadcrumbs
3/4 C. panko breadcrumbs
2 oz. mozzarella, cubed
2 T. olive oil

In a medium bowl, combine rice, ricotta, 1 egg, artichoke hearts, salt, pepper and 2 T. Italian breadcrumbs. Set aside. In a small bowl, whisk one egg. In another small bowl, place remaining breadcrumbs (both types). In the palm of your hand, form a ball with 1/4 C. rice mixture, placing a cube of mozzarella in the center. Dip the rice ball into bowl with egg, and then transfer to bowl with breadcrumbs and coat well. Repeat the process to make 8 rice balls. Heat 1 T. olive oil in a large skillet over medium heat. Place 4 rice balls in skillet and cook on all sides for a total of about 10 minutes. Remove from heat, add remaining 1 T. olive oil and repeat with remaining rice balls. Serves 4.

A great way to use leftover rice. These can be made with or without artichokes. If you only have one type of breadcrumb, use whatever you have on-hand.

# Working It™

## splurge

- 86 Chocolate Cherry Graham Deliciousness
- 87 PB&J S'mores
- 88 Bread "Pudding"
- 89 Mock Tres Leches Cake
- 90 Cinnamon Mascarpone Pound Cake
- 91 Roasted Pears with Dark Chocolate
- 92 Easy Apple and Blackberry Pastry
- 93 Brown Sugar Bananas with Walnuts
- 94 Shirley Temple Pudding
- 95 Dessert Granola

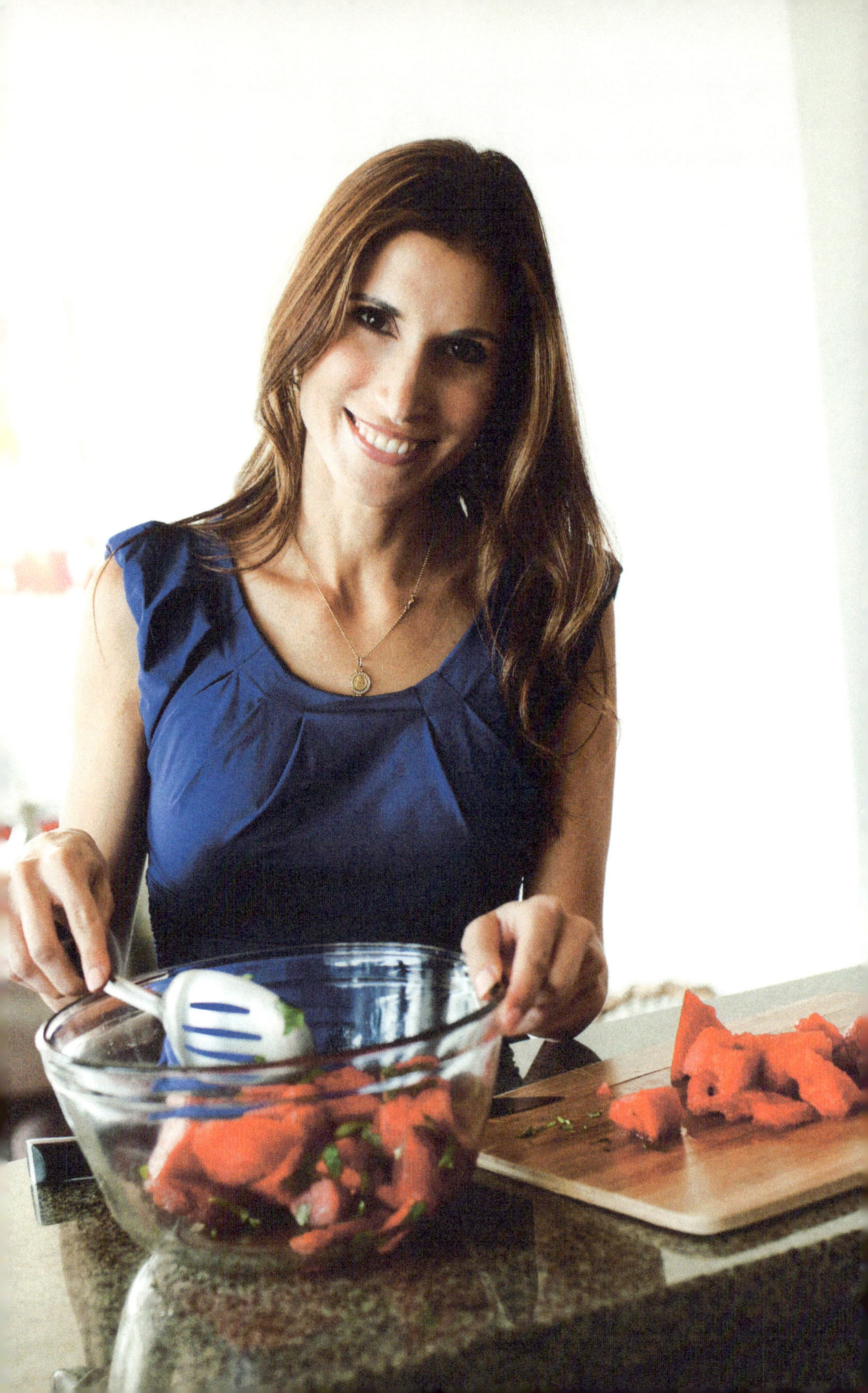

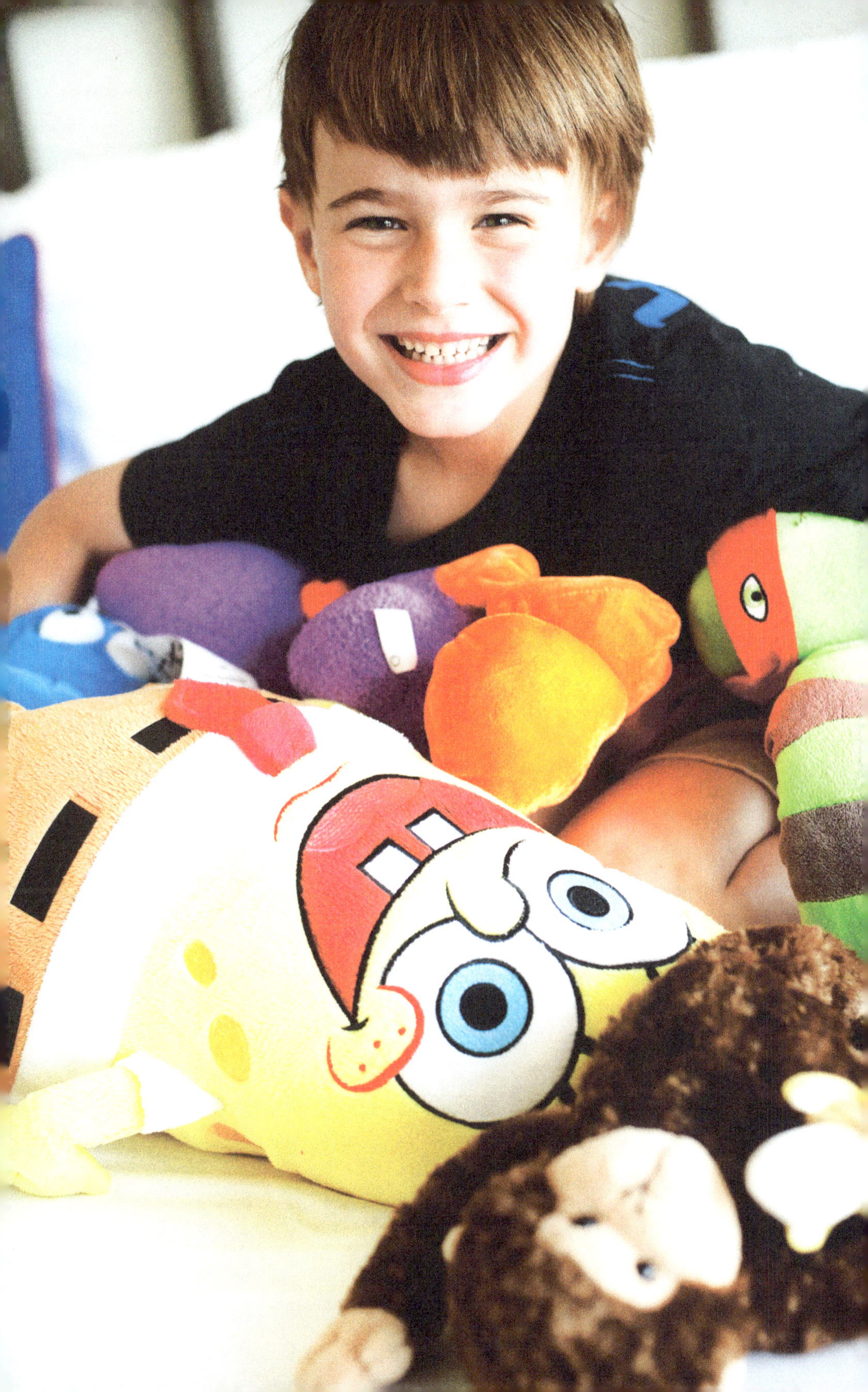

# OMG. Enough said.

## Chocolate Cherry Graham Deliciousness

**Ingredients**

**four full graham crackers**
**1 C. cherry pie filling**

**1/4 C. semi-sweet chocolate chips**
**1/4 C. sweetened condensed milk**

Preheat broiler. Place four 3″ ramekins on baking sheet. Using fingers, break graham crackers coarsely into pieces, and place one per ramekin. Layer 1/4 C. cherry pie filling into each on top of graham cracker. Then add 1 T. of chocolate chips to each ramekin and drizzle with 1 T. of sweetened condensed milk on top. Place the baking sheet in the oven for 3-5 minutes until golden and bubbly. These are best warm from the oven but can also be served at room temperature.

Serves 4.

I love this dessert! It works for an evening on your own or when you're entertaining friends. If you like cherries and chocolate, you will flip over this. Yum!

*PB&J done right.*

## PB&J S'mores

**Ingredients**

two full sheets of graham crackers
2 T. peanut butter
2 T. strawberry preserves

1/4 C. semi-sweet chocolate chips
1/4 C. mini marshmallows

Preheat broiler. Break graham crackers into halves and place on a sheet of aluminum foil. Spread 1 1/2 t. peanut butter over each half, then add 1 1/2 t. preserves over top of each half. Drop 1 T. chocolate chips on each followed by 1 T. marshmallows. Place under broiler for approximately 45 seconds until marshmallows are golden brown.

Serves 2.

A decadent weeknight treat...delicious!

## Bread "Pudding"

**Ingredients**

four baguette slices, 3/4" thick
cooking spray
2 T. ricotta
1 T. plus 1 t. dried apricots, chopped

1 T. plus 1 t. walnuts, chopped
2 t. honey
sea salt (optional)

Preheat broiler. Place bread slices on a baking sheet. Spray both sides of bread with cooking spray. Place under broiler for 1 minute. Flip bread and cook for an additional minute. Remove pan from oven and spread 1 1/2 t. ricotta on top of each bread slice, add 1 t. apricots and 1 t. walnuts. Drizzle 1/2 t. honey over top of each slice and return to broiler for 45-60 seconds. Sprinkle with sea salt (optional).

Serves 2.

You can also use any dried fruit and nut that you have on-hand. This dessert is mildly sweet and can even be served as an appetizer.

*Although "mock", it's really good.*

# Mock Tres Leches Cake

**Ingredients**

two slices of angel food cake (each 1/8 of cake)
1 T. sweetened condensed milk
1 T. evaporated milk
1 T. heavy cream
1/2 C. whipped cream
1/8 C. blueberries

Place angel food cake slices on a plate.  In a bowl, combine sweetened condensed milk, evaporated milk and heavy cream.  Drizzle the milk mixture evenly over cake, rotating the cake around to absorb the liquid.  Let sit 10 minutes.  Top each piece with half of whipped cream and blueberries.

Serves 2.

A lighter version of tres leches that takes 10 minutes to prepare instead of 4 hours. That's a trade-off I can live with!

## Cinnamon Mascarpone Pound Cake

**Ingredients**

two 1/4" slices pound cake
1/4 C. mascarpone
1 t. honey

1/8 t. cinnamon
1 T. pecans, chopped

Preheat broiler. Place pound cake on a sheet of aluminum foil, and put under broiler for 60-90 seconds until golden. In a small bowl, combine mascarpone, honey and cinnamon. Dollop half of the mixture over top of each slice. Sprinkle each slice with 1 1/2 t. pecans.

Serves 2.

A simple tasty dessert that looks beautiful.

**Fruit for dessert? Indeed.**

# Roasted Pears with Dark Chocolate

**Ingredients**

one pear, such as d'anjou
2 T. maple syrup
1 t. vanilla extract

2 T. orange juice
one square of dark chocolate
(approximately 1/10th of a 3.5 oz. bar)

Preheat oven to 400 degrees. Peel pear and cut it in half. Remove the core from both pieces and place cored-side up in an 8"x 8" baking dish. Pour maple syrup and vanilla directly over top of pears, allowing them to soak in the flavor. Add orange juice to the bottom of pan. Place in oven for 12-15 minutes until pears are tender. Remove from oven and spoon pan juice over pears. Break the chocolate square in half and place a piece in the center of each pear half. Return to oven for 2-3 minutes, remove from oven, and spoon juices over pear one more time.

Serves 1-2.

Orange and chocolate make this roasted pear a sinfully good treat.
Eat plain or with whipped cream, yogurt or ice cream.

Easy as pie.

## Easy Apple Blackberry Pastry

**Ingredients**

store-bought piecrust
one apple, such as honeycrisp
3/4 C. blackberries

2 T. brown sugar
2 t. honey

Preheat oven to 425 degrees. Cut piecrust in half, reserving half for another day. Cut remaining half into quarters and place on ungreased baking sheet. Slice apples very thinly and layer a few slices over each piece of piecrust. Add a few blackberries, sprinkle 1 1/2 t. brown sugar, and then drizzle 1/2 t. honey over each piece. Bake for 10-12 minutes until crust is lightly browned.

Serves 2.

Weeknight pie? Yep.
Serve as is or with a dollop of whipped cream or ice cream.

**Your daily dose of potassium.**

## Brown Sugar Bananas with Walnuts

Ingredients

1 T. butter
2 T. brown sugar
1 T. orange juice

two bananas, sliced
3 T. walnuts, chopped
1/2 C. vanilla yogurt

Melt butter in a small non-stick skillet over medium heat. Add brown sugar and let cook for approximately 1 minute until bubbly. Add orange juice and stir well. Add bananas and walnuts to pan, and toss gently to incorporate into mixture. Let cook approximately 30 seconds and remove from heat. Place 1/4 C. yogurt into two small serving dishes or glasses. Add half of banana mixture over top of each. Serve immediately.

Serves 2.

You can also serve with ice cream to make an outstanding sundae.

*Cheers to the cherry.*

# Shirley Temple Pudding

**Ingredients**

one 3.4 oz. box cook-and-serve vanilla pudding
2 C. low-fat milk
2 T. plus 2 t. maraschino-cherry juice
1/2 C. whipped cream
2 full sheets of graham crackers

Prepare pudding according to package instructions using 2 C. milk. Remove from heat when finished and pour evenly into four bowls. Drizzle 2 t. cherry juice into each. Using a spoon, gently swirl the cherry juice through the pudding. Top each bowl with 1/8 C. whipped cream and 1/2 sheet graham cracker. Best if served warm.

Serves 4.

Add cherries on top for extra fun!

# Crunch this.

## Dessert Granola

**Ingredients**

1 1/2 C. rolled oats (not quick serve)
1/4 C. butter, melted
1/4 C. apple sauce
1/8 C. maple syrup
1/4 C. brown sugar

1/4 C. coconut flakes
1/4 C. pistachio nuts, shelled
1/3 C. semi-sweet chocolate chips
cooking spray

Preheat oven to 350 degrees. Place oats in a large bowl. In a small bowl, combine melted butter, applesauce and maple syrup. Add mixture to oats and combine thoroughly. Mix in brown sugar. Add coconut, pistachios and chocolate chips, and stir. Prepare baking sheet with cooking spray. Add oat mixture across pan in a thin layer. Bake for 10 minutes. Remove from oven, toss gently with a spatula, and return to oven for an additional 20 minutes.

Serves 6.

Try other toppings, such as raisins, peanut butter chips and dried cranberries.

Life is a glorious dance of rapture and sorrow, and each one of us feels its inflections at various points. Good moments are like molten chocolate cake, best when you dig into the core; richness so wonderful that you never want it to end. Sometimes those moments can come in the smallest packages – a treasure hidden in your pocket that no one else can see. Other times, they are in the form of momentous achievements, like earning a degree, having your baby enter the world, or fulfilling your greatest passion.

The dance is such that there is always a twist to the side. A move that can leave you out of sync and off-beat. In those times, despite your greatest efforts, the soufflé has fallen and the kitchen is a mess. I have stood on that dance floor, as everyone has or will do, and wondered how I reached this corner of the room. Winded and shaky, I turned to lean on my fellow companions, and yes, an occasional spoon.

Food, or rather "comfort food," can truly be a tool for self-preservation. I am not talking about macaroni and cheese, and fried chicken, however. Sure, they can be like a good anesthetic that numbs unwanted pain. Real comfort food strengthens you from the inside out. It nourishes depleted cells with lasting power the way pasta fuels a runner before a long race. Not a luxurious one-time day-at-the-spa kind of pampering (which is not a bad thing either), eating well sustains you; it rebuilds whatever is broken, and it maintains the foundation.

No matter how perfect life seems from the outside, no matter how rhythmic the dance, everyone of us is vulnerable. I have learned from experience – been knocked breathless by the invisible. Food, rest and support from others can be a faithful trinity in these moments. So eat well. Cook often. And offer real comfort food to others in their times of need.

In food, there is power.

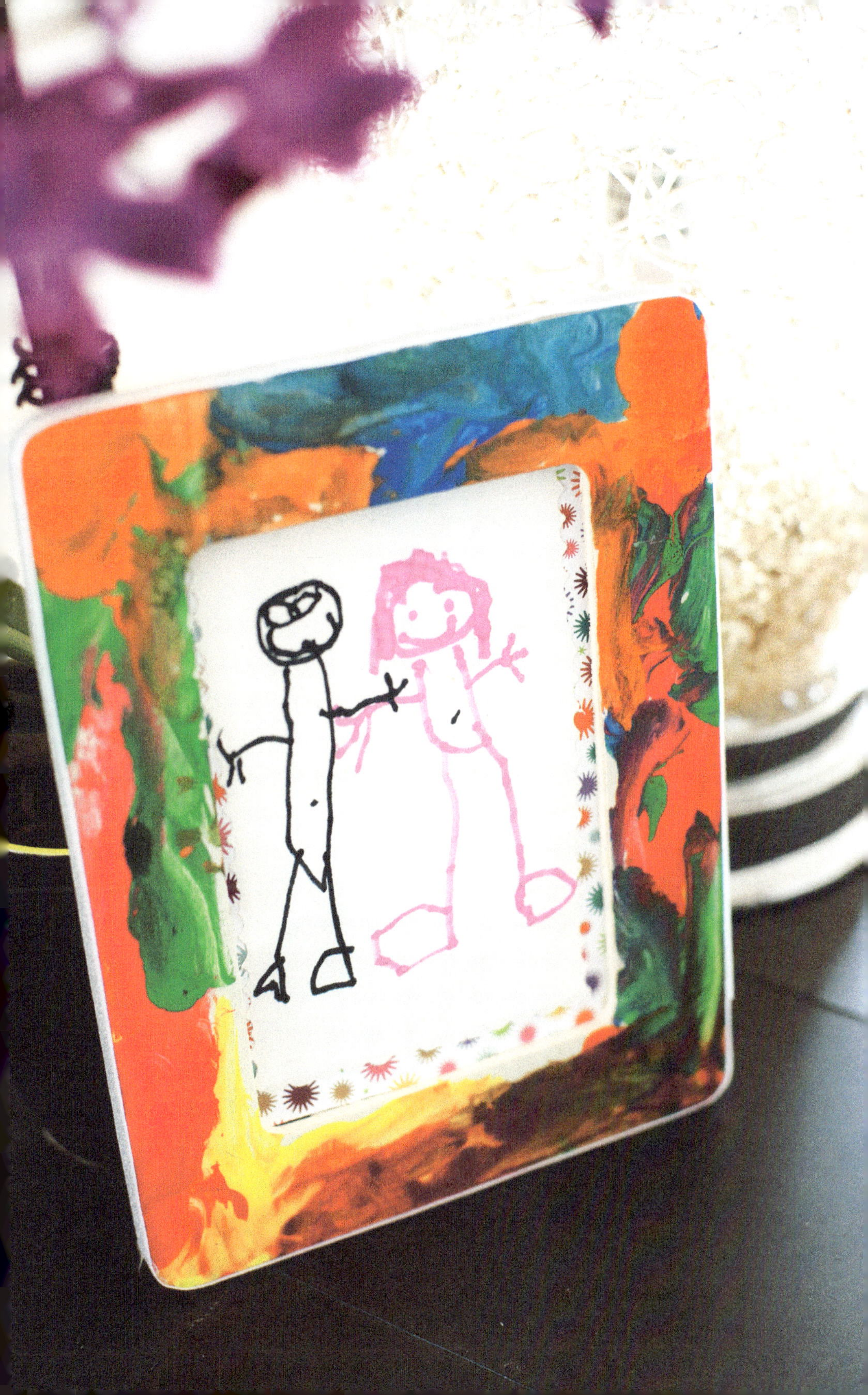

**And so, another beginning...**

Thank you, Mom, for unwavering encouragement and, Dad, for providing a life of wonder.

To my sisters, together we dance in rain and in sunshine.

Kim's affinity for the kitchen began with Julia Child cooking shows when she was just a young girl. She learned and practiced with her grandmother, an Italian woman made of steel who worked as a hospital dietician and crocheted hats for a living. Kim pursued corporate life but never gave up her passion for food. In 2004, she launched her first food company, conducted demonstrations aimed at corporate professionals, and held in-store tastings at retailers, such as Crate & Barrel. She has been featured in regional and national news outlets, including Fox Business News, Lucky magazine, Work magazine, The Richmond Times Dispatch and Newsday, among many others.

Author, Kim Baker

Many of these recipes were inspired or shared with me by the wonderful people that have crossed my path. To all the smiles that have graced my life, I say thank you.

To find out more, visit facebook.com/kimbakerfoods.

CPSIA information can be obtained at www.ICGtesting.com
Printed in the USA
LVOW02*2304270215

428445LV00007B/11/P

9 780990 669203